CROSS COUNTRY
SKI INNS

Northeastern U.S. & Quebec

Mountain Top Inn, Vermont

CROSS COUNTRY SKI INNS

Northeastern U.S. & Quebec

BY MARGE LAMY

Designed and Produced by
ROBERT REID and TERRY BERGER

A **SNOW VACATIONS** BOOK

NORTH RIVER, NEW YORK

Front cover photograph: Edson Hill Manor, Stowe, Vermont.

All photographs not credited are by George W. Gardner.

Text copyright © 1991 by Robert Reid Associates.
Photographs copyright © by George W. Gardner and credited photographers.

Published by Robert Reid Associates, New Haven,
for *Snow Vacations Books*, North River, New York, 12856.

All enquiries and book orders should be directed to the Trade Distributor:
INLAND BOOK COMPANY INC.
P.O. Box 120261
East Haven, CT 06512
(203) 467-4257
FAX: (203) 469-7697

A Robert Reid / Terry Berger production.
Typeset in Trump Mediaeval by Monotype Composition Company, Baltimore.
Produced by Mandarin Offset, Hong Kong.
Printed and bound in Hong Kong.

LIBRARY OF CONGRESS CATALOG CARD NUMBER: 91-066371

ISBN 0-9630607-0-8

CONTENTS

INN THE BEGINNING . . .

THIS BOOK is the brainchild of inn owner George Heim. Soon after buying Garnet Hill Lodge at North River, New York, in 1977, he observed how important was his listing in *Country Inns and Back Roads,* by the Berkshire Traveler, the late Norman T. Simpson, Jr. Later, Garnet Hill Lodge was discovered by Robert R. Reid, producer of the Country Inns of America series, and was included in one of those well-known regional editions, all illustrated with four-color photographs.

Within ten years, George had developed an outstanding cross country skiing center at the inn, and he realized that a separate guide for winter travel was needed. He took his idea to Reid, who agreed to lend his graphic design skills, and professional contacts.

To help in searching for full service inns with a special interest in skiing, George called upon his fellow innkeeper, Joe-Pete Wilson, former Olympic and world competitor in nordic skiing and bobsledding, and who was a pioneer in the cross country skiing business. As the co-author with William J. Lederer of *Complete Cross Country Skiing and Ski Touring,* Joe-Pete couldn't believe he hadn't thought of a book on ski inns himself.

Both men traveled thousands of miles checking out good locations. They wanted to offer a range of possibilities—quaint and elegant hostelries, groomed and ungroomed trails, developed centers, and back country terrain. For the writing they found Marge Lamy, a skier and former weekly newspaper editor in Lake Placid, New York, who has written for years on the Adirondacks, travel, winter sports, and history. The first edition appeared in 1986.

This new edition has also been produced by Reid, a bi-cultural, Canadian-American designer of books and newspapers, who began the *Country Inns of America* series under the aegis of *Architectural Digest.* He has since published books on dude ranches, hunting and fishing lodges, and preserved railroads. His partner, Terry Berger, author of children's books and other inn books, has served as editor of this book.

LINKING GOOD INNS TO GOOD SKIING

LIKE A CHINESE GONG that continues to resonate, subtly changing intonation long after it is struck, a good country inn stays in the mind, to be recalled again and again. A fine meal, a view, a cozy room, or some physical feature may be what makes it memorable. A friendship may have developed, or perhaps an attachment to a town or a region. Newcomers to inn travel claim such discoveries change their lives, opening up new opportunities for enjoyment.

The most devout skiers may consider the trails or the kind of terrain first, but then experiment until they find the right inn for them. It is not surprising that in conversation around the dinner table or fireplace, the same names keep coming up, linking a good inn to good skiing.

The majority of winter travelers, however, consider the inn first. They seem to explore a bit, but once they've found the combination they like, they return as often as they can. If the snow conditions are not ideal or the weather is unfavorable, cross country skiers can find other things to do, such as hiking or scouting crafts and antiques shops.

To enhance that experience—and shorten the search—we have tried to give a sense of place in the descriptions that follow. A bit of history, something of the personalities involved, an idea of the facilities available—all help the traveler to make a rewarding decision. **7**

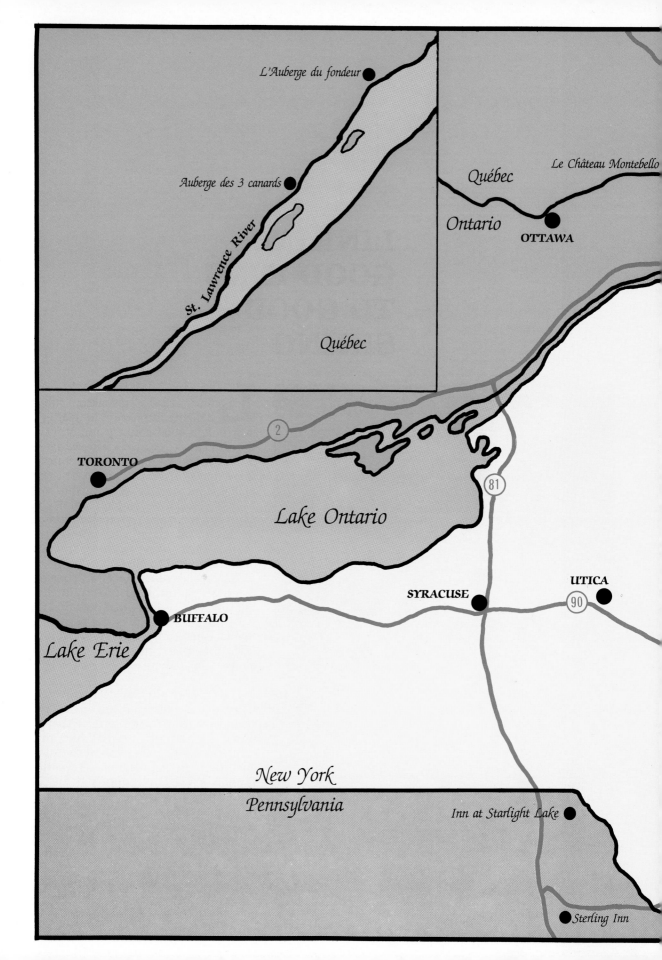

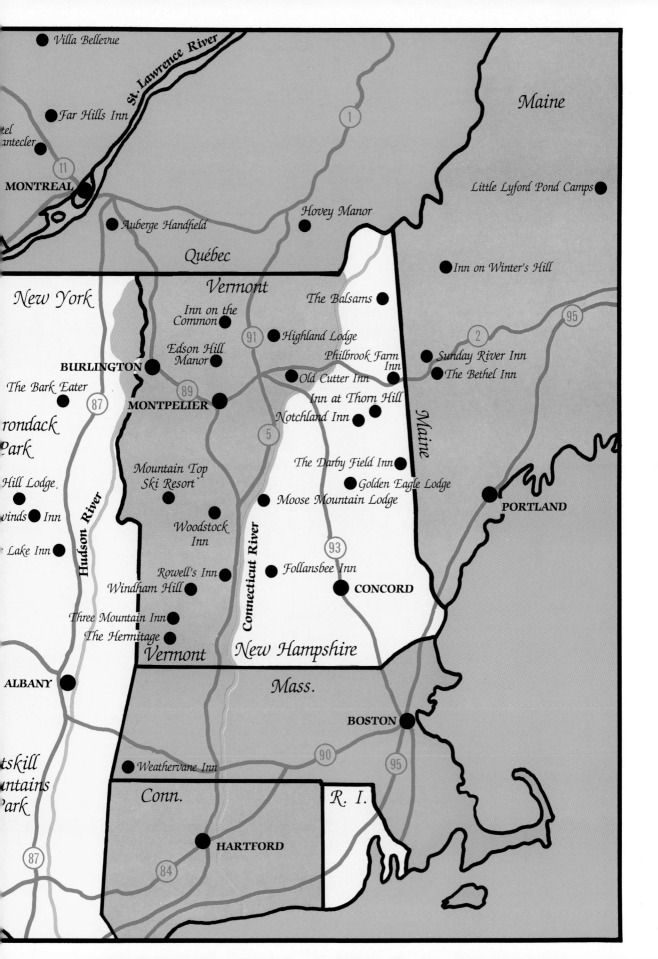

New York's Adirondack Mountains viewed from ski trails at Garnet Hill Lodge.

PENNSYLVANIA
NEW YORK
MASSACHUSETTS

Many of the comfortable guest rooms have fireplaces.

THE STERLING INN

The jewel of the Poconos

THE STERLING INN has created its own village green, just around the corner from the Poconos community for which it is named. Many of the cottages in the complex, post-Civil War homes, were built when the area thrived as an agricultural center and when a silversmith's active trade in New York and Philadelphia made it renowned for its sterling.

Inn owner Ron Logan, former history teacher and sometime lecturer in that field, feels the name of the town can probably be attributed to the combination of favorable attributes the area enjoys. Being located close to large eastern cities has to be one of them.

The inn is a most happy blend of agreeable features, pleasing layout and architecture being foremost among them. The original part of the main building, dating from the turn of the century, was built by one of the village's founding families, large enough to permit them to take in "summer boarders" who followed the railroads everywhere. Each addition to the inn is anchored by a huge, natural stone fireplace replicating the first one. Overhead, bedrooms are supported on huge beams.

The last addition is a glass-enclosed, 18-by-36-foot swimming pool with Jacuzzi and greenhouse. Changing rooms are tucked behind the adjacent bar, which serves as the connector to the inn.

Two large rooms provide dining space, proving the popularity of the

The inn's dining room attracts guests on its reputation for fine cuisine.

*The scenic bridge
over Wallenpaupakack Creek.*

SKIING AT
THE STERLING INN

The milder quality of the Poconos winter beckons visitors into endless activity. A ride in the horse-drawn sleigh for two is especially popular with couples (the inn gets a lot of honeymoon and anniversary couples). Skating on the lake is great family fun, day or night. Chestnuts roasted over an open fire are available at rinkside.

There are trails for both walking and skiing on the inn's 103 acres, so that snow supply is no problem. A guidebook is provided for the mile-long nature trail that climbs the ridge opposite the inn. The Falls Trail, a mile each way, crosses the fast-running 19-Mile Run, above where it joins the Creek near the inn. A number of picnic sites are located along both trails.

Ski trails circle the top of the ridge, through a mix of tree cover, with one loop through a patch of high blueberry bushes that have taken over an old orchard. The ridge, about 2000 feet in elevation, is deceiving because of the lie of the land, but it offers a good workout.

Longer, packed trails can be found a few miles away at Tobyhanna State Park, where a ranger's office supplies maps and advice about trail conditions. In the opposite direction is the intriguing "Promised Land" to explore.

The inn has its own ski shop, with rentals and instruction, plus hot soup, drinks, snacks, and waxes. Tanglewood is only one of a half dozen ski centers within 30-minutes' drive where the inn can arrange for discount tickets.

inn's kitchen. Another clue lies in the number of menu choices; everything is created here, from breads and rolls to delectable desserts.

Most guests choose to "dress for dinner," although the letter that greets them merely requests jackets for gentlemen. Jeans-wearers do not feel uncomfortable, especially in winter, when casual dress seems more the order of the day.

The "front parlor" is formal in décor but divided into seating arrangements that encourage relaxing over a cup of tea in the afternoon, a cocktail, or an after-dinner drink. Next door is the Terrace Room, large enough for dancing on weekend nights in high season, or for a meeting.

Both these common rooms are lined by bookshelves, and a quiet corner can always be found. Most guest accommodations are suites and many rooms have fireplaces.

A recently renovated cottage behind the inn has sliding glass doors leading to a deck overlooking the Wallenpaupack Creek.

Ron feels that country inns are the most effective combatant for today's high-tech world. "If anything," he says, "they probably will become more inviting and popular as society marches on to higher technology."

*The inn's 103 acres have many ski trails, some for serious skiers like the one shown above, right.
The horse-drawn sleigh is very popular, below, right, and everyone enjoys the heated indoor pool for its physical relaxation and striking setting.*

THE INN AT STARLIGHT LAKE

Five-star hosts

On the trail in full regalia.

A BIG, natural-stone fireplace on one side of the living room and a wide, cast-iron stove with footwarmers and a Rube Goldberg chimney on the other instantly seduce anyone entering the Inn at Starlight Lake in winter. But an even greater attraction in pulling people back again and again, to this tiny enclave nestled in the hills of the upper Delaware River Valley, are hosts Judy and Jack McMahon.

Still, the McMahons do not feel they dominate life at the inn. Even though it is also their home, they feel the personality of the place is established by their guests.

A cross-stitched sampler in the inn proclaims "The blessing of the house is contentment." On a quiet night in midweek, the guests may gather to read by the fire, to chat quietly in the sun room, or to watch the sole TV. On a weekend evening, on the other hand, a feature-length film may be playing to a full crowd in the game room. Concur-

rent competitions may be running on both the pool table and the shuffleboard table in the game room. Yet another group may be clustered around the grand piano in the main room, and in the bar next to it.

Everyone starts off the day with a multiple choice breakfast, served in the solarium fashioned from part of the front porch that once ran the full length of the rambling building. Overlooking the lake and literally dripping with plants, the room conjures up images of how pleasant the summers must be.

Back in 1909 when the inn was built, it was strictly a summer retreat for wealthy escapees from the heat of Philadelphia, New York, and New Jersey cities. Vacation homes built in the intervening years, many still held by the same families, have kept the lakes in a kind of suspended animation, resisting the development that can change an area's character. Thus it remains a restful and rural setting.

The inn's sizable dining room accommodates the part-time residents as well as day-trippers who drive in to ski or just to have lunch. In recent years, outdoor clubs have discovered the inn for excursions that often begin with breakfast. Rather than interfering with the service to house guests, the outside business helps the inn maintain an extensive menu.

Since the McMahons took over the inn in 1974, they have modernized bathrooms and renovated extensively, both the inn and the cottages. The rooms in the main house are decorated in a more traditional way, with much of the original furniture still in use. The hallways are lined with wonderful old prints and paintings.

One of the cottages has been made into a modern, two-room suite with

A trademark of Starlight Lake is the fine food served in the relaxed atmosphere of its dining room.

fireplace and double Jacuzzi. Another resembles a split-level house with cozy, low-ceilinged bedrooms and open living spaces.

The appeal of the inn crosses all age barriers, says Judy. Surely that reflects the owners' gracious hospitality as well as easy access to the outdoors.

SKIING AT THE INN AT STARLIGHT LAKE

Two broad ridges rise on each side of Starlight Lake, from a 1400 feet elevation at the ski shop to 1800 feet at their highest points. Directly behind the inn, the trail zigzags along a short, steep incline and passes one of the quarry sites that sent bluestone slate to pave the streets of New York in the last century.

"Top-o'-the-World" circles the crest through open hardwoods; other loops traverse the meadows on the brow of the hill with views of rolling countryside. A longer trail dips into a shallow valley around Rock Pond.

Lights . . .
Camera . . .
Action . . .
an exciting part
of cross country
skiing.

Alongside the skating rink cleared in front of the inn, skiers cross the lake to the network that begins from the opposite shore. Open meadows and an apple orchard offer space to slide around and practice snowplows. At the bottom of this slope and around the corner from the inn lies the tiny village.

The outer perimeter of trails winds over the ridge, leaving behind the open fields, and dipping down along steep ledges on the north side. At the far end of the ridge, a stiff climb labeled Yes-U-Can (in case anyone wants to try going down), opens up views of farmland to the east. A series of loops on top of the ridge provide an endless test. When snowcover permits, a long trail runs from the back of the ridge around Hempstead Lake.

For alpine skiers, a number of well-known Pennsylvania ski centers are within easy driving distance of the inn. And even in winter, guests can go hunting for antiques.

Left, innkeepers
Judy and Jack McMahon.
Right, the inn
from across the lake.

18

The award-winning dining room, above, is noted for its fine wine cellar and wine-tasting dinners.

Left, the attractive guest rooms are fitted with iron, brass, and carved wooden bedsteads.

FRIENDS LAKE INN

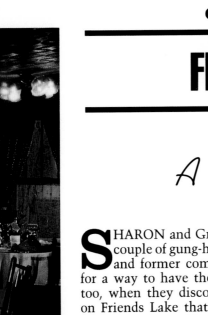

A mecca for good food

SHARON and Greg Taylor were a couple of gung-ho downhill skiers and former competitors, looking for a way to have their sport and eat, too, when they discovered an old inn on Friends Lake that had been closed for some time. After a short try at running a tutorial training program for young racers, they decided to return the inn to its original function.

Close to the Lake George region at the eastern edge of the Adirondack Park, the location has always been important to the inn's success. The Taylors have capitalized on their market by making the inn a mecca for good food, too.

The five-course, nouvelle cuisine dinners have received rave reviews from food editors in the Albany Capital District. One magazine cited the inn in its 1990 awards as first in ambience and runner-up as best all-around restaurant;

the inn was runner-up as well in three individual categories: best appetizer, best meat entrée, and best service. Not bad for a country inn competing with city restaurants and some of New York state's best resort hotels!

The 19th century dining room contributes to one's eating pleasure, with its walls of golden chestnut wood, slender columns, pressed tin ceilings, and a fine view of the lake. An unusual double fireplace and bookshelves line the rear wall with windows defining the outer walls. At the front of the house the veranda has been enclosed for a bar.

The inn was first a boardinghouse for workers in the nearby tanning factory, and once post-Civil War prosperity arrived, it served transient travelers. It prospered so well that by the turn of the century the owners, the Murphy family, had to expand it. The inn played a prominent role during the rum-run-

The inn is located close to Lake George in Adirondack Park.

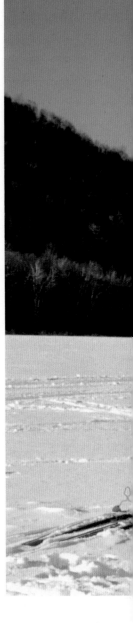

ning days of Prohibition, and the Taylors are still hearing tales from guests who knew it in those days.

Most of the bedrooms are the size one would expect to find in a country inn, but some are very generously proportioned. The Taylors have remodeled and added baths (some with whirlpools) so that none of the rooms seem cramped. They are attractively fitted with iron, brass, and carved wooden bedsteads covered with old-fashioned coverlets.

On the main level, a spacious foyer is ample for people arriving back from skiing or coming in for a meal. A large living room on the opposite side of the dining room, also faces the lake. It has tables for games or cards, a piano, a television set, and a wood-burning stove. A glass display case highlights some of Greg's competitor's awards.

The Taylors have developed a fine wine cellar and conduct wine-tasting dinners, with an overnight special rate. These are held between fall and spring. Half a dozen murder mystery weekends, in which guests play assigned roles, are also sprinkled throughout the quiet season.

SKIING AT FRIENDS LAKE INN

Most of their guests are "pretty action oriented," the Taylors report. If so, they are well matched with their energetic hosts, who slip away whenever possible for an hour or an afternoon of skiing.

The land behind the inn is deceptive, for it looks low, but soon after entering the woods with only a little climbing and a few dips and doodles, the skier discovers that the trails lie on two parallel ridges with a wide gully between them. There are about 20 kilometers of tracked and groomed trails, with possibilities for more leading in three directions.

Most of this is intermediate skiing, in predominantly conifer forest. A few short climbs add spice to the offering, combined with some long, steady downhills.

Across the road from the inn, a short road leads to the inn's property on the lake. A wooded greenline has been maintained around it, sheltering the vacation cottages and homes. From this access point, beginning skiers can practice or make the 7-kilometer circle around it.

Long trips into backcountry areas can be taken on state lands, but a guide is required and can be provided by the inn for a fee. One easy and picturesque trail along the banks of the Hudson River begins at a bridge just a few miles from the inn.

The Gore Mountain Ski Center (alpine only) is ten miles away, and there are commercial ski touring centers within a convenient distance as well.

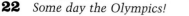

Some day the Olympics!

This couple has been caught
having a rest break and
a spot of lunch at the
edge of the frozen lake.

HIGHWINDS INN

An inn with a view of spectacular sunsets

During the daytime, there is a good view from the terraced dining room.

Below, left, one of the four guest rooms.

"TELL ONLY your best friends," advises the brochure for Highwinds Inn. It should add, ". . . and then bring them!" What a perfect place for a house party.

Highwinds was built as a residence in the thirties by the Barton family, who have owned the garnet mines on Gore Mountain for more than a century. Later used for vacations and company meetings, it opened as an inn in the mid-eighties.

Only the skiers atop nearby Gore Mountain Ski Center can enjoy the view that Highwinds guests do . . . and they must leave at the end of the day, when the sunsets make it most spectacular.

From the inn's 2500-foot elevation, the highest peaks of the Adirondack Park range across the northern skyline. Westward are the borders of the Siamese Ponds Wilderness Area and beyond that, Snowy and Blue mountains. Gore's summit is another thousand feet above and behind the inn. On a clear day, the sun rising over Gore first tints the crests of these distant peaks and then spreads pink and orange hues down their sides, gradually deepening the blue of the sky.

The weather show can be viewed from the windows of the dining room, an enclosed porch off the large living room. A red garnet stone fireplace at one end and a standing, stuffed bear at

A group setting out from the inn for a day's skiing.

25

*Cross country skiing
involves a certain amount
of UPhill skiing.*

for the long run back down to the village. "Ride Up, Ski Down" was the slogan for the hundreds who poured off the ski trains each weekend.

Today, inn guests make the long climb up from the shores of the Hudson River the easy way, by car . . . and then they remain. At this elevation, there is a great deal more sky to see than in most other places, and at night, far from any competing lights, it can be awe-inspiring. Indeed, the spectacle is always worth the price of admission.

SKIING AT HIGHWINDS INN

Between the roads built for access to the mines and logging, and trails to the top of Pete Gay and Gore mountains, there is something here for all. In addition, an overland trail connects into the extensive trail system at Garnet Hill Ski Touring Center.

Several trails with great views follow the roads that wind around the mountain near the inn at easy grades for beginning skiers. Open areas around a pond below the ski shop and the private airstrip offer more space for practice.

Longer trails in the intermediate category climb higher to explore a shallow plateau some distance above the inn. All are groomed wide enough for ample turning and checking on hilly parts.

The overview on the side of Pete Gay is pleasant for either skiing or snowshoeing. The more demanding climb to the top of the mountain leads to a housekeeping cabin, one of two for rent year-round, an eagle's eyrie where only fuel is provided and everything else comes in on one's back. The long descent is a real kick.

Hardy telemark skiers can climb to the new runs on Gore operated by the Olympic Regional Development Authority and buy a ticket to use the gondola and chair lifts there. Others will make the round trip to enjoy the wider views from the other side of the mountain into Vermont.

About 30 kilometers of trails are groomed. Strong skiers can use additional ungroomed trails, including the Siamese Ponds Wilderness Area. Highwinds is one of the inns on the backcountry tour that traverses that area.

the other are the dramatic elements in the main common room. For additional space, there is a game room with pool table downstairs. The kitchen is always accessible to guests and space is afforded to store food for lunches.

With only four bedrooms, this is a very intimate setting. Innkeeper Kim Repscha is as solicitous as if the inn were her own and she transmits a very personal feeling to her guests.

In spite of its small staff, the inn can accommodate up to 40 diners, and many who come to ski for the day plan to remain for dinner. There are at least four appetizers and five to six entrées on the menu at all times. All the baking is done on the premises; homemade ice cream is a specialty. Herbs from Kim's large vegetable garden and jams from blueberry and raspberry bushes on the grounds delight guests all year long.

Back in the thirties when North Creek opened its first downhill ski center at the "skibowl" outside the village, the Barton family cleared a hill near the inn on Pete Gay Mountain and set up a tow. Then they fostered the
idea of busing people up to the mines

The view from the summit of *Pete Gay Mountain, 3100 feet up. There are two housekeeping cabins at the top of this mountain, from which the view can be enjoyed in the warm confines of a firelit interior.*

The ski shop is the center of a 50 km cross country trail system.

Dinner can be enjoyed in the firelit dining room or on the porch, with its scenic vistas.

GARNET HILL LODGE

A traditional Adirondack lodge and ski touring center

AROUND the turn of the century, a small mining village, complete with store, school, and three-story boardinghouse, developed at the garnet deposits Frank Hooper found near 13th Lake. By the twenties, the garnet had run out, and the Hooper family converted the former miner's quarters into a resort for summer tourists.

Lovely as this tiny valley was, the real gem, they discovered, was the spectacular view from the top of the hill overlooking the lake. In 1936, they built the Log House, still the heart of Garnet Hill Lodge, in the style of an Adirondack camp—mammoth in size, with hewn beams and rafters, and a front porch running the full length of the house.

George and Mary Heim have expanded the inn considerably since 1977, when George retired from the Navy and they brought their family to the Adirondacks. They have improved the lodge, added and remodeled cottages in more modern décor, and created a kitchen famous for its excellent cuisine. The jewel in the crown for George is the cross country center he's developed, now celebrated as one of the East's finest.

There seems to be a continuous flow of people around the lodge, some heading for the trails, which start outside the door, others mingling by the fire to compare notes on their latest excursion or coming in for a snack and a warming cup.

A red garnet fireplace dominates the high-ceilinged main room of the lodge. Heavy, handmade furniture is arranged around it. The other side of the long room is dining space; these tables are popular in the evening because of the fire, but in the daytime, the enclosed porch is favored. There is a sitting area at one end, the ideal place for relaxing on a stormy day with a book.

The lodge sits at 2200 feet above tide, therefore the mountains surrounding 13th Lake may not appear terribly high.

Saturday night buffet at Garnet Hill.

Larry Wilke assisting a guest in the store.

But the inn takes every advantage of the view: the Heims now have nine balcony rooms with sliding glass doors and individual porches. Pine paneling and the original period furnishings give the interiors a thirties look.

Two small cottages near the inn offer more privacy: one recently renovated has whirlpool baths and a separate lounge. Guests can also have a taste of staying in an authentic Adirondack "camp," Big Shanty, the Hooper family manor, situated closer to the lake and directly on the trails leading to it. Rustic furniture, twig and birchbark trim, and a fireplace that looks as if it could hold up the earth are only part of its charm.

The menus at Garnet Hill are as hearty as ever, but Mary has adapted them to the new preference for healthier eating. A low fat menu and vegetarian choices are always included in the entrées, which incorporate veal, chicken, and fish. Outside diners have to drive a long way to reach the lodge, but their numbers are a testimonial to the excellence of the kitchen.

A small room off the living room has a ping pong table, and a full-size pool table is set up at the end of the common room near the entrance. At the opposite end of the building, the library offers yet another space, where the lone TV is located. Special movies and activities are often featured at the ski shop in the evenings.

SKIING AT GARNET HILL LODGE

The guests who come to Garnet Hill take their sport very seriously. And well they should. The ski center has grown to match the traffic, with 50 kilometers of trails, a new and larger warm-up room, and a separate lounge for season-ticket holders upstairs. The snack bar serves soup, chili, and pizza, plus hot and cold drinks; day skiers can have lunch at the lodge.

Sloping away to the east from the inn and the abandoned mining site lies a network of trails designed to be taken in large chunks or small. There is plenty of space for beginners to practice, including the frozen lake and, next to it, a wilderness trail that once was an old farm road. Novice trails have names like 4-H, E-Z Way and Porcupine Path.

Several longer runs in the more difficult category follow the landfall of Balm of Gilead Brook. A round trip on Cougar Run, Coyote Pass, or the Trapper Trail will provide a very good workout. It's even more fun to enjoy the mostly downhill romp and take the ski center shuttle bus back to the lodge.

George has steadily improved and enlarged the system; top competitions are held every year, along with training for professional instructors. Garnet Hill pros hold teaching clinics using video for guests during the week.

All the trails are tracked and groomed and most are wide enough for skating. A couple of wilderness trails are left untouched.

This is one of the principal entry points for the Siamese Ponds Wilderness Area, where there are miles of untracked, backcountry trails. The lodge also participates in a guided, inn-to-inn tour that traverses part of this area.

The inn building has changed over time but the stunning view varies only with the seasons

Meticulously groomed trails complement the surrounding wilderness.

The inn, above, was once an old stage coach stop.

The former carriage house, left, now contains four guest rooms.

BARK EATER INN

An Olympian is your host in ski country

THE SENTINEL RANGE stands duty over a small glacial valley that forms one of the passes through the mountains between the AuSable Valley and the plains of North Elba where Lake Placid is located. Around the turn of the century, Joe-Pete Wilson's grandparents worked for a lumber company in winter that ran the largest operation on the Placid side of the range, he as farrier and driver, she as a camp cook. At the same time his great-grandparents worked at one of Lake Placid's most famous hotels, the Stevens House.

Today, Joe-Pete carries on the tradition at the country inn his parents established in the 1940s over the mountain in Keene. While some guests still come just to relax and enjoy the scenery, as they did in an earlier day, more come to participate in the sports he revels in . . . cross country skiing, hiking, climbing, and horseback riding.

Collecting antiques is another of Joe-Pete's passions, and the inn is chock-a-block with them . . . not just furnishings but tools, and trivia, and whimsey as well. Wherever the eye turns, there is something of interest.

The main inn was built in stages, beginning with a small farmhouse characteristic of the region in the early years of the 19th century: A roomy kitchen where guests are encouraged to visit and a small dining room are located on the ground floor of this section, and a bedroom and bath overhead. A two-story bedroom wing was later added.

The inn was a meal stop at various times when the stagecoach line ran between Lake Champlain and Lake Placid, depending on whether there was a good cook in the family. This traffic prompted the first major addition, a large dining room whose cobblestone fireplace is the focal point. A mixture of mahogany furniture adds warmth to the room, and dinner is served here family-style.

The last addition came with prosperity, an adjacent living room with another natural stone fireplace. Stay-at-homes and returning skiers share it

The guest rooms are named for animals. This is the Chipmunk Room.

equitably. Upstairs there are more lodgings.

Bedrooms vary in size, but all have plenty of windows and carefully chosen furnishings that distinguish them. Inn guests share two baths. The carriage house next door has four double rooms with private baths, and on the hill behind the inn is a log cottage with two complete apartments.

Breakfast doesn't quite come up to lumberjack standards, but the chef sends everyone off prepared for some kind of activity. That may be as non-taxing as shopping in Lake Placid or seeking out regional crafts people.

Dinner must be reserved before leaving for the day; outside diners are accommodated only if the house count permits. The menus at the Bark Eater are legendary now; entrées are limited, but that has never affected the number of repeat visitors. Soup, salad and dessert are the accompaniments, all homemade, as are the crusty breads.

SKIING AT THE BARK EATER

The Bark Eater lies in a sheltered valley in the lee of the High Peaks; in recent years of uncertain snow supply, its trails have not always been skiable. Cross country skiers, being flexible, will switch to hiking or horseback riding, for which there are even more trails. On the inn property are two low hills separated by meadows with many fine views.

Just over the pass through the Cascade Lakes on the main highway, the Mount Van Hoevenberg Sports Complex has 50 kilometers of groomed and tracked trails and a ski center with complete services.

Peter, a member of the hard working kitchen staff.

The Olympic Regional Development Authority also maintains the Olympic bobsled and luge runs there; training takes place daily with competition and public rides on weekends. Hockey, ski jumping, figure skating, and speed skating events are part of the winter program that has been conducted in Lake Placid since the turn of the century.

Joe-Pete maintains a small ski shop with gear for rent and purchase, guides, instruction, and waxing assistance. He and his staff can suggest any number of wilderness trails, from climbs in the High Peaks to the St. Regis Canoe Area.

The beginning of the long-distance Jackrabbit Trail travels through the old stagecoach route toward Lake Placid. Guests can ski it to reach the Mt. Van Hoevenberg network or be ferried to the upper end for a long slide back. Good intermediate skills are needed.

Several other touring centers operate in the area. Whiteface Mountain Ski Center is only a few miles away.

Innkeeper Joe-Pete Wilson, a former Olympian, shown skiing with his sister, Marge Lamy, who is the author of this book.

The inn sets a fine table.

THE WEATHERVANE INN

A family affair—
nestled in the Berkshires

There are ten attractively furnished guest rooms, some in the main house and some in the carriage house.

VINCE and Anne Murphy can trace the history of their inn back through 19 owners to the very end of the 18th century. Although a fire destroyed the town records, on the back of their menu is a reproduction of an 1876 map of the town that clearly identifies the inn.

At first this was a prosperous agricultural community with a charcoal industry and marble quarry. Later factories made chairs and cannonballs. Then the trolley lines were extended from Great Barrington and the village turned into a thriving resort. South Egremont is still a gem, listed on the National Register of Historic Places, and showing less change from the impact of the automobile than many a Berkshire town.

The Murphys found the inn when they came to ski at nearby Butternut Mountain. Although Vince insists he had no intention of owning an inn, Anne whispered in his ear every night. In 1980 it became their home and a family undertaking as well. Their daughter, Patricia, worked with them for eight years after they bought it and their son, Bob, and his wife, Olena, have joined them now.

"When Irish Eyes Are Smiling," could have been written for Anne. Her sunny disposition is evident everywhere, from her welcoming smile to the cheerful curtains and quilts she makes for guest rooms.

There are ten guest rooms. Divided between the main house and the carriage house, they range from a handsome master bedroom with fourposter bed and fireplace at the front of the inn, to two more conventional rooms on the lower level in an addition that opens directly onto the lawn and swimming pool area.

Two large, Victorian-style "front parlors" are connected by a high archway. One has bookshelves, a game table, and television set. A graceful walnut staircase with curved balustrade adds elegance to the front foyer.

Another spacious sitting room at the center of the house, next to the formal dining room, is a popular gathering place because of its fireplace. There is a small bar adjacent to it that operates during the day on a chit system.

Breakfast is served in the Garden Room at the rear of the inn. A skylight and windows overlooking the tree-lined lawn make it bright on the stormiest winter day.

Dining is an important part of a stay at the Weathervane, and chef Anne Murphy attempts to satisfy all palates

Anne and Vince Murphy are the innkeepers, and operate the inn with the help of their son and daughter-in-law.

JULIE JUBIN PHOTOS

37

with an innovative menu that offers a choice of six or more appetizers and entrees. The chef also caters to vegetarians, and can concoct some palatable alternatives to her regular dishes. The luscious, homemade desserts appeal to everyone.

The inn does take outside diners by reservation; in winter dinner is served only on weekends. Late arrivals can call to have something saved or to exchange the Friday night meal for Sunday brunch. These are famous in the district, especially Mrs. Murphy's corned beef hash.

SKIING AT THE WEATHERVANE INN

Residents of South Egremont can be seen daily walking through town with their skis on their shoulders heading for the golf course, which is a long stone's throw from the inn. There are also within walking distance open meadows at the edge of town. More exacting terrain requires driving.

Massachusetts has its own Mount Washington and in the town named for it, adjacent to South Egremont, is the Mount Everett Reservation. A 5-kilometer road, once used for cars in summer, makes easy work or a 900-foot climb to the summit. From its 2600-foot elevation are views of the Housatonic Valley to the west and this corner of the Berkshires on the east. Heavily timbered earlier, the public land of the reservation is now covered with large, second growth maple, beech, oak, and elm.

From the same town highway, the more demanding Ashley Hill Brook Trail, about 11 to 12 kilometers, covers more varied terrain, partly through a pine forest, leading to a 2150-foot elevation.

Butternut Mountain has a small cross country area combined with its alpine services, and there are a number of small commercial centers not far away. Beartown State Forest at Great Barrington and the 10,000-acre Pittsfield State Forest have extensive free trails without services.

For more companionable skiing, the Murphys recommend Kennedy Park in Lenox and the Pleasant Valley Wildlife Sanctuary, near that community, operated by the National Audubon Society. Both have marked trails, maps, and scenic sites.

Many of the rich cultural resources of the region can be enjoyed in the winter too.

The inn is surrounded by many skiing areas, from the local golf course to Butternut Mountain to the Beartown and Pittsfield state forests.

Originally an 18th-century clapboard colonial house, with later additions.

The White Mountains of New Hampshire.

VERMONT
NEW HAMPSHIRE
MAINE

THE HERMITAGE INN

The inn, which offers a variety of skiing opportunities for all levels of skiers.

For connoisseurs of good living

The incomparable wine cellar of innkeeper James McGovern. Jim's advice for a dinner wine should be taken seriously.

JIM McGOVERN has a whole bevy of gentlemen's hobbies—collecting fine wines, prints, and antiques; raising rare birds and English hunting dogs; and shooting. Fortunately, they all combine beautifully with keeping a country inn . . . and his guests are the beneficiaries.

Many return regularly just to check the additions to Jim's wine cellar. Every year since 1984, he has received the

Grand Award from "Wine Spectator" for having "one of the greatest wine lists in America." He has built his collection to over 40,000 bottles representing more than 2,000 labels, some of which are available in his wine shop.

Probably the menu should come next in any discussion of The Hermitage Inn. Suffice it to say that it is one of the best-known dining places in the Wilmington-Mount Snow area, offering a varied and substantial list of entrées. The kitchen staff are real pros and Jim and his wife Lois stay attuned to changes in food styles, while still incorporating the timeless favorites of a New England inn.

The dining room extends the full width of the inn at the rear, with windows on three sides, including one in Palladian style that faces Black Mountain. The raised ceiling accommodates Jim's gallery of Delacroix prints; he now owns all but one of the original 160 pieces. They line every wall, competing for space with part of his collection of 400 to 500 duck decoys. Some are for sale.

Jim and Lois have spent years searching for the distinctive antiques and fine prints that fill each room in this 18th century farmhouse, owned at one period by Bertha Eastman Berry, who edited the Social Register. Many guest rooms have fireplaces and all have private baths.

The innkeepers can be found doing any one of a thousand chores around the place during the day, but the ready companions are the dogs, who are so relaxed that they bely their training for the field. Outdoors, they seem sublimely unaware of the pheasants, geese, wild ducks and wild turkeys raised for the table in nearby pens.

43

*Telemark skiing
is becoming more
and more popular.*

Jim conducts a release program in season on the 1000-acre hunting preserve surrounding the inn, where he offers guided hunts and dog training. Sporting clays, a target-shooting game, has been added to the winter entertainment.

The popular gathering spot at The Hermitage is the cozy bar and lounge with fireplace in the center of the house, between the dining room and a porch that was enclosed for serving lunch. Other inn buildings with sitting rooms include the Wine House, attached to the main building, the Carriage House, and Bound Brook Inn, where pine paneling and a stone fireplace add appeal.

SKIING AT
THE HERMITAGE

In winter, the ski shop takes over the front of the wine shop. Tickets, rentals, waxing, hot or cold beverages, and professional instruction are dispensed as required. Advice is free.

Cross country skiing has come a long way since Jim cut the first trails here in the early '70s, just after taking over the inn. They had to beg people, give them the skis and throw in free fondue, just to get them to put on those silly skis!

Today guests find everything from a teaching area, a few loops in the woods right around the inn and a trail to the Mount Snow airport and golf course for beginners to a norpine trail on top of the mountain. The latter involves riding the Haystack Mountain Ski Center lifts to the ridge behind the inn and skiing the 6-kilometer trail along its spine. An annual race is held here, but it's more fun to go slowly and take in the magnificent views of the flatlands west toward Bennington and east toward Brattleboro.

For the myriad of skiers of medium ability, there is the remainder of the inn's trails. The Cold Brook Trail, labeled intermediate, climbs to part of the same ridge and then gives an exhilarating ride down on logging roads through open hardwoods. One can return to the inn or try an expert loop back over the ridge, intersecting Cold Brook.

A larger section of trails lies on a low ridge across the town road, part of Jim's hunting preserve. This is also the route to the Catamount Trail. The inn trails are groomed and tracked with special equipment pulled behind snowmobiles.

The dining room, besides its exquisite cuisine, exhibits Delacroix prints and a collection of duck decoys.

WINDHAM HILL INN

Gourmet dining by candlelight

KEN and Linda Busteed like to call their cross country facility "a learning center," but actually the whole experience of a stay at Windham Hill Inn is a lesson in living well. From surroundings pleasing to the eye to sumptuous food beautifully presented to the accoutrements of the good life like fine china and silver, and service that is attentive without being overbearing . . . this is a rare treat.

The white-washed brick of the 1825 farmhouse has faded to a pale pink cast that softens its lines. Five rooms have been constructed on the front side of the barn, some with sliding doors; the hay mow alone is large enough to hold concerts in summer.

When the Busteeds bought it ten years ago, the house was a challenge to Linda's talents as a professional interior decorator. The bedrooms, all with private baths, are spacious enough to make them comfortable, inviting retreats.

Each has been given a distinctive personality, using architectural features in an interesting way, and the original wide plank floors are preserved.

Rooms are named for members of the original owner's family and for leading figures in the town's history, among them the forebears of the William Howard Taft family, who settled in West Townshend at the end of the 18th century.

Two sitting rooms in the main part of the inn are formal yet welcoming; one has a fireplace and the other, a stove. The sun room, which seems to be all windows, and is done in more modern dress, with white wicker furniture adding to its airiness. On all sides the serene view of broad meadows is outlined by low mountains.

Breakfast is served in a small alcove at the rear of the house, a room enlivened by the half-frame of an 1890s sleigh used as a wall sculpture. Dining

Innkeeper Linda Busteed sets a beautiful table. The elegant dining service and crystal is from the original family.

by candlelight at the mahogany table in the large dining room becomes one of the dramatic highlights of one's stay for it is with the six-course gourmet dinners that one's education truly begins. The choices are amazing, considering that Ken and Linda share the chef's duties.

Windham Hill was named one of ten "Best Inns of the Year" nationwide in 1988–89 by Uncle Ben's Country Inns. The award is made by a panel of judges from the industry, based on excellence in cuisine, service, ambience, and fine innkeeping. It made a fine anniversary present for Ken and Linda's tenth year at the inn.

Ken and Linda find that their guests have changed over the years: couples now outnumber families and cross country skiers outnumber downhill types. But there are alternate pastimes for all of them, like checking out antiques and craft shops or visiting Townshend, which has a rich historical past.

SKIING AT WINDHAM HILL INN

Windham Hill is actually a shoulder of Turkey Mountain, so the Turkey Trot is a very appropriate name for the upper trail that climbs through a mixed grove of trees above the inn. Buck Rubbins is the lower loop in the same woods, leading to the Trot. Both take advantage of the terrain without requiring heavy duty climbing.

Ken has expanded the trail network, intended for their guests' use only, because of the growing numbers of skiers. The new section on the hill, called Longmeadow, lies on an open field next to the woods with even better views of the surrounding mountains than from the inn. It is groomed in wide swaths where one can practice turns or learn to handle a little speed.

The cleared fields around the inn are still used primarily for instruction; the inn has a professional instructor on hand who will make excursions with guests, as well. Longer tracked loops called Ken's Kruise and Picnic Run have exciting downhills, too, because all the landscape tilts toward the valley.

Down along the West River lie some very attractive, skied-out trails. The valley floor widens downstream where repeated floods carved out high bluffs long ago. Wild turkeys are more likely to be sighted by skiers along these sheltered banks than up on the mountain in winter.

Any number of commercial ski centers are located in this area, but the Busteeds find that their guests have a more laidback approach. Getting some good exercise is only one part of the equation, and these trails do just fine.

Guest rooms are named for family members and leading historic figures in the town, giving each room a distinctive personality.

With the inn in the distance,
the skier enjoys a run on
cross country ski trails
that range over land that
once comprised a prosperous
farm.

*Innkeepers
Ken and Linda Busteed*

49

*The centerpeice of
a charming Vermont village,
Three Mountain Inn
is the quintessential
Vermont inn.*

THREE MOUNTAIN INN

An inn with a soul

SOME INNS tug at the heart strings as soon as one enters, evoking an immediate connection with the past. Three Mountain Inn is one of these.

The entrance from the parking lot leads first through a low-ceilinged room that serves as a small pub. Next is the main common room, the heart of the house, where pine exposed ceiling beams are set off by 24-inch eighteenth-century pine panels darkened by age. The room is lightened and enlarged, however, by a wall of large-paned windows.

Magic seems to emanate from the fireplace in this charming room and although not large, it draws the eye constantly. It contains one of the house's two historic beehive ovens.

Charles and Elaine had no idea when they bought the inn how important it was to be located just down the road from Stratton Mountain, although the previous owner was one of its founders. Both were mid-westerners, Elaine from Ohio and Charles with roots in Michigan, where his family had owned a summer hotel on Mackinac Island.

They were working in Manhattan in photo-journalism and banking when this change occurred.

Preserving this charming old house was a primary concern. Long-time residents applaud what they've done. Extra bedrooms with cozy, low ceilings were installed in an attached section once used for woodshed and barn. A neighbor told Elaine, "I used to pick up my milk here."

The small-scale "front rooms" facing the street are used for dining. The "library" contains the other beehive oven fireplace, also framed by wide paneling. Windows look out on two sides, and half moon arches add graceful touches over the bookshelves. In the matching room on the other side, wood trim provides interesting detail.

The intimate feeling carries into the guest rooms, although most are spacious and have ample sitting room and window space. Furnishings of proven age and workmanship are chosen to suit a room without overwhelming it. In addition to ten rooms in the main inn, there are six next door in Robinson House, which has a conference room

The guest rooms, one of which is shown at right, have wide-plank floors and period furniture that contributes to the colonial ambience of the inn.

51

with spectacular views of the mountains. Sage House, another early home across the street, is generally rented to families or groups.

Another attraction is the food. Here again good fortune has thrown another superb chef, Elaine, in the path of a lot of lucky travelers. To kitchen klutzes, it is almost scary to find three to five appetizers, three to eight entrées (on weekends), and three to five desserts coming from the small space she commands.

In 1981, three years after Elaine took over, the inn was cited for its "small but first-rate menu" in "Playboy's Guide to Ultimate Skiing."

SKIING AT THREE MOUNTAIN INN

Although the mountains in southern Vermont are dotted with notable alpine centers, there is equally good opportunity for cross country skiing, both on public land and at private centers.

The entrance to Jamaica State Park is just down the street from the inn, past the village skating rink and across the bridge over the West River. A novice trail goes in both directions, but the more interesting tour goes upstream.

This stretch of the river is famous for white water racing in spring, and the state also is trying to re-introduce salmon. The trail swings away from the water from time to time, and at other places is squeezed onto a narrow shelf overlooking the stream. Views of ledges and mountains on the other side are dramatic.

There are two brooks to cross on ice, one with a waterfall above, before reaching Cobb Brook, which is large and not

always frozen. Using this as a destination, the round trip will be about ten kilometers, but the intrepid can explore further. Other untried trails lead off from this one.

A more rugged trek of 15 kilometers from West Wardsboro to Stratton Pond is rated intermediate-expert. This is back-country skiing, with Mount Snow behind and Stratton Mountain ahead on the way in. Part of the trail overlooks Somerset Reservoir.

For groomed skiing, the favorite with most guests is Wild Wings, a family-oriented center deep in the woods near Peru, about 25 miles away. It has easy trails, high views, a warming hut where lunch is served, nice informality, and instruction.

The Sun Bowl at Stratton Mountain can be reached by a back road from Jamaica.

The Jamaica State Park is just down the street from the inn, and has novice trails going in several directions. Back country skiing to Stratton Pond requires more expertise. But at the end of all that skiing, there is always a warm and welcoming fire on the hearth back at the inn, below.

ROWELL'S INN

Pure Vermont, inside and out

ROWELL'S INN is one of those places that ought to be viewed from a horse-drawn sleigh or a vintage car. Sitting as it does on a bend in the road between Chester and Londonderry, it deserves much more than a passing glance from travelers whizzing by in today's vehicles.

No one needs to produce credentials to prove that the inn belongs on the National Register of Historic Places. The Greek Revival style brick building is a fine example of an unusual recessed gable style found in the Connecticut Valley, Vermont, and occasionally in New Hampshire.

Major Edward Simon built the inn in 1820 as a stagecoach stop for the town he created and named for himself.

Fortunately, the inn has now fallen into the good hands of Beth and Lee Davis who are expert at extending to guests a true inn experience.

The past takes over as soon as one opens the door; the place overflows with historic detail. Two reception rooms balance the front entranceway, with stairs leading to the upper floors. Guests register in the room to the left, where there is a panel of mailboxes that replicate the old post office.

The dining room in the center of the inn is the largest public room. It was modernized in the early part of the century, when the Rowell family added cherry and maple floors. Portraits of Beth's ancestors lend benign benediction from heavy Victorian frames, matching the era of the patterned tin ceilings.

Beth concocts her magic in a surprisingly small kitchen tucked between the pub and the dining room. She offers fresh, hearty country fare, using her own family recipes. She has been featured in magazines for her cooking.

Guest rooms on the second floor are laid out symmetrically, flanking the central stairway. Fireplaces and carefully selected period furniture add to the feeling of having stepped into the past. Blown-up old postcard scenes have been hung in the hallways.

A winding staircase leads to the third level, formerly a ballroom, which has been divided into two bedrooms with curved, vaulted ceilings and sleigh beds. Furniture original to the house has been

Beth Davis putting the last touches on the table settings in the dining room, where her country cooking from old family recipes is served.

The inn has been furnished with pieces left from the Rowell family, combined with other pieces restored by the innkeepers, Beth and Lee Davis.

There are a number of ski centers around the inn, ranging from novice to difficult. The trail at right through the woods could appeal to anyone, however.

restored and original bath and light fixtures retained where possible.

SKIING AT ROWELL'S INN

Rowell's Inn is a destination for both skiing and walking inn-to-inn tours. Part of the walking route between Simonsville and Andover, unused in winter, is adapted for cross country skiing. From it, one can circle through neighboring fields and explore an old cemetery.

Directly behind the inn, a trail connects with Viking Cross Country Center, an uphill challenge only for those in good condition. The downhill trek back, preferably with a guide from the center, is recommended. It crosses a number of neighbors' lands and is skied out by the center staff for the tours.

The drive to Viking, high on a hill outside of Londonderry, is roundabout, but the setting is beautiful. The 40 kilometers of trails dip into valleys and explore forest and field. The center has a warming hut with café and outside deck, a skating rink, and a 2-kilometer lighted track for night skiing. Instruction is available.

Wild Wings Touring Center near Peru is a farm set in the woods with a barn converted for warming shack and services. Trails have been cut out on National Forest lands by the local outing club; about 15 kilometers are groomed and five are primitive skiing. They also offer instruction. This is a more family-oriented center, according to Lee and Beth, and is very popular with their

guests. *It has the best elevation to receive snow supply, and breathtaking views.*

Tater Hill is the closest developed center, on a high plateau, where a potato farm has been converted to a golf course. The trails are novice-rated, extending from the open meadows to gently rolling forests surrounding them. The clubhouse offers refreshments, socializing, complete services, and instruction.

WOODSTOCK INN AND RESORT

A premier inn with a premier ski touring center

THE colonial design of the Woodstock Inn blends well with the 17th and 18th century houses that line the famous elliptical green of Woodstock, one of Vermont's most beautiful villages. Behind the serene facade of the hotel, much has occurred.

A major expansion in the past few years to give the inn an all-season appeal seems to have infused president and general manager Chet Williamson's staff with a new spirit. It is only the latest transformation in the series of hostelries that have preceded it since Richardson's Tavern opened in 1793.

Early in the 19th century the inn flourished as the community did, adapting to the changes from farming, forestry, and small indigenous industries to serving the tourist trade. Following the Civil War, and the return from California of Frederick Billings, a native son who'd made his fortune as a San Francisco lawyer during the Gold Rush, the town received a major boost.

Having been involved with the Northern Pacific Railroad, Billings built the small line that ran between White River Junction and Woodstock. Traffic was so good that the inn, then called the Eagle Hotel, had to be replaced. Townspeople raised the money to build the new hotel, which opened in 1892.

An early innovation was the golf course, which took over the cow pasture on the hills above the present country club. A winter sports center operated at the golf club in 1910. By 1912, a ski jump was added to the 1000-foot, torchlit toboggan run; sledding, snowshoeing, skating and skiing were all part of the fun. Therefore it is not surprising that one of Woodstock's enterprising sportsmen developed the nation's first rope tow in 1934. Two years

Woodstock Inn is a premier cross country ski touring center, with tracked and groomed trails and an indoor sports center with every facility you can imagine.

If there is someone special in your life, this is the place to spoil them.

The Common Room, and its massive stone fireplace, decorated with folk art.

later it was moved to the present Suicide Six, which became one of New England's most popular alpine centers.

Changes in travel threatened the inn's survival in the 1960s, until local leaders persuaded Laurance Rockefeller, who was married to Frederick Billings' granddaughter, to add it to his resort holdings. In 1969, the present inn was built, behind the former one directly on the green.

Ample space and balance in design carry over from the outside to the interior. A ten-foot fireplace is the focal point of the main common room and a corridor leading to a new wing encloses shops and a solarium that overlook the atrium stairway to the lower level. A pianist entertains every afternoon in the solarium while tea is served. French doors lead to the gardens, which are also visible from the semi-circular addition to the dining room.

Richardson's Tavern has been relocated to the new wing and enlarged with booths, fireplace, and a wall of windows. Three separate townhouses extend south from the Tavern Wing. Guest rooms include four suites with fireplaces, built-in book cases in sitting rooms, and enormous baths. Handmade quilts and handloomed coverlets are admired for their beauty as well as for comfort.

A tour of the newly-renovated kitchen is part of the weekly schedule. Chef Peter Wynia, who has been at the inn for 21 years, is rightly proud of it.

Wynia labels his menus "Regional Alpine Dining," a soupçon of offerings from other countries and regional American dishes. He features locally-produced lamb and veal, fresh pasta, and pastries made on the spot. His buffets are legendary. Informal dining is available in the Eagle Café, which commemorates the former inn.

SKIING AT THE WOODSTOCK INN

The Woodstock Country Club, a five-minute walk from the inn, still converts from golf to cross country skiing in winter. The club has a fully outfitted shop, storage and waxing room, changing rooms with showers, and restaurant with fireside lounge. The golf course is used for instruction, and skiers can move across Kedron Brook to the adjacent Mount Peg trails as they improve.

Most of these are intermediate level, though they lie on the side of a fairly abrupt hill; one trail climbs about 300 feet to an overlook with picnic bench. There are also some advanced trails here.

Mount Tom stands guard over the town on the north, facing the inn. On its north slope lies an extensive system of wide and gentle roads built on the Rockefeller estate for carriage driving and logging. All are groomed and tracked trails.

There are two especially scenic destinations. One high over the village at 1250 feet looks over the Ottauquechee River. Guided tours, including lunch, can be arranged to a log cabin which has a big, welcoming woodstove.

All of the 60 kilometers of trails are tracked and groomed, some for skating.

The Courtside Restaurant at the Sports Center, a mile from the inn at the far side of the golf course, is another alternative for lunch. Inn guests use the center without charge. Ski facilities and equipment are gratis except for weekend and holiday periods.

Skiers can work out tight muscles in the 60-foot lap pool or relax in the whirlpool, get in a racquetball or tennis game or have a massage. Aerobics and fitness classes are offered, too.

RIGHT, the formal dining room, with some of its elaborate cuisine set out in a buffet.

MOUNTAIN TOP INN AND CROSS COUNTRY SKI RESORT

Bring the whole family . . . there's lots to do

A NEW MINDSET begins to take hold as soon as the traveler reaches Chittenden Village, crossing the iron bridge and passing the statue to the town's war dead, presided over by the town hall and a few modest dwellings. There are still a few miles to go . . . up and up to the broad shelf of land that overlooks Chittenden Reservoir from the west. Not until one enters the inn does the full impact of the setting register, dramatically highlighted by the glass-enclosed silo staircase opposite the entrance.

Comfortable furniture divides the broad lobby of the inn into sitting areas, one around a handsome fireplace. The south lobby also sets off the view to good advantage with a wall of windows. White wicker furniture and a few whimsical antiques add to the effect. Tables for games and puzzles and comfortable divans for reading are provided

A first-class ski center complemented by a luxurious inn with breathtaking views. Left, the inn's dining room; left, below, a corner of the ski shop; right, the ski center where everybody starts off.

and a small TV room stacked with videos is tucked away around the corner.

The dining room on the lower level was built long and shallow so that the magnificent view predominates. Exposed ceiling beams, a crackling fireplace, and Canadian snowshoe chairs render the interior warm and inviting.

Bill Wolfe and Bud McLaughlin, the Mountain Top management team, are brothers-in-law carrying on a family tradition. "We feel this is our home," says Bud, "and we want people to be at home here." They are constantly extending new offerings, to make the inn a complete destination resort without losing the inn spirit.

Bill and Margery Wolfe, Bill's parents, established the business in 1945 when they bought the farm from a wealthy philanthropist, who had converted the barn into a wayside tavern as a hobby

JERRY LEBLOND PHOTOS

for his wife. The Wolfes entertained President Eisenhower on a fishing expedition in 1955.

By 1963, they decided there was enough ski business to justify staying open in winter. Three years later, with the aid of Rudi Mattesich and the New England Ski Touring Council, they cut out cross country trails on National Forest land nearby.

In 1977, fire destroyed most of the inn, when deep snow blocked firefighters. Bill and Margery rebuilt, trying to recreate the Yankee integrity of the original building. Two, 12-inch by 16-inch, Douglas fir trusses run the length of this building, visible from the interior. Gradually, the family replaced the antiques lost in the fire, but that accounts for the slightly more modern furnishing in the guest rooms. All have private baths, sitting areas, and a comfortable country look. There are additional rental units in outbuildings.

Casual dress is acceptable in the dining room, which serves basically American food with strong New England influences. There are many choices and the cuisine is a source of pride. There is a cocktail lounge next to the dining room, which has live entertainment on weekends.

Some guests find the sauna and whirlpool a delightful way to unwind. The game room, with ping pong and billiard tables, is favored by the younger set.

There is a flooded rink outside the inn (skates can be supplied) and sleigh rides that go on runners or wheels. Special events like art instruction, golf school, and mystery weekends are scheduled throughout the year.

SKIING AT MOUNTAIN TOP INN

Mountain Top Inn has spent 25 years building one of the premier cross country try skiing centers in the East. Its unique snow-making system, pioneered by center director Don Cochrane, guarantees at least two and a half kilometers of skiing, almost without regard to general weather conditions. In addition, the meadows above the inn are mowed as closely as a lawn in summer, so they're skiable with very litle snow.

This kind of care plus 110 kilometers of trails varying in length and difficulty have won the center a strong following. This is a skating paradise, with 40 kilometers of double-tracked trails, most of them 12 feet to 15 feet wide.

The ski shop has ample space on two levels, with a great wood stove for cold days and an outdoor deck for warm ones. There are three warming huts on the trails.

Don keeps up with changes in equipment and carries a full line of gear; his staff can give expert advice for individual needs. There also is a large staff of certified professionals.

Feeder paths fan out in four directions to relieve traffic at the shop. The teaching area has been moved to big open meadows away from the inn.

The difference in elevation alone, from 1495 feet at the reservoir to just under 1800 at the inn and 2175 on top of the mountain, guarantees a good test of ability. The only black diamond trails are limited to a couple on the mountain and a long one around the reservoir. Other challenging terrain is available on adjacent National Forest lands.

*Left,
Guests relish the flying saucer ride down the hill in front of the inn.*

Right, the view from the dining room doesn't always include a skier, as shown here. Right, below, the signs indicate how well-marked the trails are.

JERRY LEBLOND PHOTOS

The old Darling Farm is now a charming inn with first-class cuisine and cross country skiing from the front door.

THE OLD CUTTER INN

Swiss know-how on Burke Mountain

THE OLD CUTTER INN is most remarkable for its excellent food. Most travelers would not expect to find such fare in a small inn tucked away in northern Vermont. The inn itself slips on like a favorite pair of old slippers—nothing pretentious—just comfort, good service, and a friendly, low-key atmosphere.

Owner Fritz Walther is transplanted from Switzerland, where his family owned a large hotel in Bern. When his father died, Fritz was too young to help his mother, so she sold the hotel, and he eventually apprenticed as a chef.

For a few years Fritz moved around, first in Europe, then to Canada and the U.S. Seasonal jobs appealed to him because he could learn different kinds of cooking, see new places, and enjoy the resort life.

He broke that pattern when he landed in Stowe, where he worked with Tony Flory, the executive chef of the old Tollhouse Inn, famous in its day. Fritz says he was the best all-around chef he'd ever known. He also met his wife Marti, who had come to Stowe to learn to ski.

Three years after they were married in 1974, they learned by happenstance that the Old Cutter Inn was for sale. They bought it, although it was a gamble, to say the least. The inn had opened and closed and changed hands, but had never become established.

Fritz knew that his cooking would be the main attraction. He was right. Inn goers were joined by others, permitting Fritz to offer an extensive menu. He features continental cuisine, and offers several Swiss specialties and a champagne brunch on Sundays.

The inn occupies what was formerly the Darling Farm, which had been revived as a working farm and summer retreat early in the century by Elmer Darling, the owner of the Fifth Avenue Hotel in New York. More recently, the farmhouse had been reconstructed to take advantage of its original charm. The dining room, for example, is divided into sections, has big beams overhead, lots of windows, and a fireplace.

One of Fritz's first moves was to enlarge and modernize the kitchen. A glass partition permits guests to see the preparations going on there . . . and of course enjoy the aroma.

To the right of the entrance is a small pub where light snacks are available. A room beyond it, with an enclosed fireplace, takes care of dining room

ARTHUR E. ROSLUND, JR. PHOTO

Good skiers start early.

67

*Innkeepers
Fritz and Marti
Walther.*

overflow. Breakfast is served there, and it makes a pleasant spot for reading or playing board games during the day.

The bedrooms in the inn are homey and befit the farmhouse setting. The nearby carriage house has additional lodgings, including an apartment, with simple but pleasant furnishings. All of the rooms have sitting areas.

SKIING AT
THE OLD CUTTER INN

The Old Cutter Inn has more than 50 km of groomed, tracked, and well-marked trails. Guests can ski down to the cross country center, operated by Stan Swaim, or they can call him to find out what is recommended for the day.

The ski center itself is a converted farmhouse with a geodesic warming hut next to it, and offers rentals and instruction. Open meadows and farm roads are perfect for beginning instruction and warm-ups. Above the inn, and spread out through old hardwood forests are about 20 km of more difficult skiing. From open areas on these trails one can see most of Northeastern Vermont. The easier skiing, mostly on old logging roads and hiking trails, is a mixture of deep woods and open fields, which were farmed until recently.

There are stretches where pine and spruce close in around the trails, making it seem secluded even when the road is not far away. Because there is so much variety in the landscape, the skier has the impression of having traveled much farther than the actual distance.

*Great skiing,
great scenery.*

EDSON HILL MANOR

Alan Alda slept here!

THE GEORGIAN COLONIAL style of Edson Hill Manor— steep-pitched, gabled roofs, and handhewn log and brick facade—has a solidity and grandeur that well match its mountainside surroundings.

Lawrence Heath, Sr., bought the estate, formerly a millionaire's retreat, in 1954 because of his love affair with skiing and his desire to bring his family to Stowe. Although it only dates back to 1940, the manor has history built into it. Some of its beams stood for a hundred years in the barn owned by Ira and Ethan Allen in North Burlington. The exterior brick came from a Burlington hotel that burned in the thirties.

The expansive living room is pine-paneled and has a large fireplace framed by comfortable divans where guests gather for tea, cocktails, or after-dinner drinks. Bookshelves line the rear walls and French windows outline the 30-mile vista.

The dining room wing was added in 1957, with great care to match the exterior. Here, too, wide windows emphasize the beauty of the natural surroundings. On the level below is the Skiers' Lounge, where snacks are served on weekends, and above, there are additional bedrooms.

Pine paneling is found throughout the manor house, along with original paintings and prints. Slanted ceilings add to the cozy feeling of the bedrooms, all of which have private baths except for one small room usually shared by a family. There are fireplaces in many rooms.

The single-story carriage houses, set above the manor and closer to the woods, are newer but similar in design. All the rooms are large and have pine-paneled `walls, beam ceilings, brick fireplaces, private baths, and wooded views.

The chef at Edson Hill offers an excellent variety of items, complemented by a fine wine cellar. There are always choices for vegetarians, and several certified heart-wise entrées in addition to nightly specials. The inn does accept outside diners.

Two comments on the same page in the guest book are revealing. One couple wrote, "First anniversary," and the second, "40th and still going strong."

The only complaint was, "Didn't see

Fred and Jim, the Belgian draft horses that make the sleigh rides a special event, especially by moonlight.

Ice fishing on the pond, either to catch trout or the Mercedes that was sunk there.

A part of the inn shown below. Another view is shown on the front cover.

71

Guests appreciate the fine wine cellar, which complements an excellent variety of dishes,

Alan Alda." Actually, the most frequently asked question is about the filming of Alda's biggest moneymaker ever, "The Four Seasons," at Edson Hill. The famous car-in-the-pond scene may be its most memorable moment; apparently it did not disturb the fish. The ponds and the stream that feed into them still are among the best natural spawning grounds for rainbow and brook trout in this area.

Eric and Jane Lande now guide the affairs of the inn with their general manager Bob Howd. They note that a surprising number of guests don't leave the property once they arrive, in spite of all the glitter of the alpine resort below.

SKIING AT
EDSON HILL MANOR

The Edson Hill Cross Country Ski Center is part of the interconnected trail system that crisscrosses the entire Stowe area. On the 500 acres owned by the manor, there are 40 kilometers groomed for skiing, five of them wide enough for skating.

There are short swings around the manor marked novice and longer loops for good intermediate skiers. One begins with Wade Path, winds east around the side of the mountain above the manor, up a steep section called Adam's Climb, and finally returns on a gentle downhill along the Old Billings Road. That the latter was a well-traveled road long ago is hard to believe now.

The Catamount Trail joins the Edson Hill trails coming in from the south. Skiers can connect in that direction with Topnotch, Trapp Family Lodge, and Mt. Mansfield networks, totalling 180 kilometers. All the centers honor each others' tickets.

Edson Hill maintains its own ski shop, with certified instructors and guides. It is located down the hill from the manor, where there are open fields and gradual slopes for beginners to practice.

There are a few advanced wilderness trails in the Edson Hill system. Others to Bolton Valley and west over Smugglers Notch will appeal to strong skiers.

The stables have 19 horses for riding, and two huge Belgians, Fred and Jim, are the draft horses for sleigh rides, available anytime but most popular by moonlight.

On the inn's 500 acres, there are 40 km of groomed trails for cross country skiing; 5 km of these are wide enough for skating.

Special tiles surround the hearth of the fireplaces in the guest rooms.

Northern Vermont is exceedingly picturesque in the winter because it gets lots of snow.

There are ten charming guest rooms and four cozy cabins.

HIGHLAND LODGE

Where guests return time and again

A RARE QUALITY of light surrounds the Highland Lodge, a combination of its lakeside setting and the open, rolling country, much of it still being used for farming, on this high plateau in northern Vermont. There is a sense of serenity from an earlier age that has left an unmistakable stamp on the region.

By the 1880s, the farmhouse built almost 20 years before reflected the flourishing life its residents had made for themselves; the antecedent of the present inn is clearly recognizable in a photo on the wall of the office. Already there had been an invasion of "summer people," who set their stamp on the town. College professors from the University of Vermont and Princeton University began buying up land around Caspian Lake; and the upper end became known as "Deansboro."

An excellent local Greensboro history, of which owner Wilhelmina Smith was a prime mover, says that, "In the early 1900s, every man who discovered his wife had a spare moment opened a boardinghouse." The 1920s was, indeed, the boardinghouse era. The Highland Lodge became the central provider for guests and residents of 76 cottage lots laid out by Vermont Summer Estates. The present kitchen wing was built and the wrap-around Queen Anne porch with porte-cochère was a useful addition.

The 1929 Depression ended the dream of a cottage colony. However, it left the inn with a first-rate tennis court and the town already had a dandy, 9-hole golf course, with great mountain views.

The inn's next good fortune was being purchased in 1953 by Dave and

Two dining rooms provide excellent dining on a wide variety of imaginative dishes.

75

Carol Smith, parents of the present owner. They ran it as a family resort and developed the beach area and playhouse. Most important, they established a warm and continuing relationship with their guests.

Dave, Jr., and his wife Wilhelmina carry on the tradition. "We've watched whole families grow up here," he observes. Dave returned in 1979 after he attended college, where he met Wilhelmina, then spent time in the Army, and practiced law. He finds innkeeping satisfying because of the direct, enthusiastic response from guests.

They have built up loyalty with their staff, too; young people pass on jobs to their siblings. Their chefs are local people whose creative talent with food they recognized and encouraged with culinary training here and abroad. It is a wise investment; the food is delicious, and menu choices are wide and imaginatively presented.

One of the trails leads to town and it's worth taking for a visit to a genuine, old-time country store—the Willeys Store.

SKIING AT HIGHLAND LODGE

Most of the sledding done in Greensboro in the early 19th century was not for sport, but for hauling farm goods to market. Later, as the Greensboro local history reports, young people made sleighs for having fun.

At first the older Smiths didn't try to stay open in winter, but in 1972 Dave, Sr., decided to get permission from neighboring land owners to lay out some trails. There are now more than 70 kilometers of them.

A small network of four to five kilometers next to the lake consists of skied-out trails through good rabbit country. There

The groomed and tracked trails are laid out to take advantage of the views.

is very little up and down except for getting back and forth from the inn, perhaps 150 feet above the lake. Many guests choose to ski the frozen circumference of the lake, where they can check on ice fishermen, too.

The most spectacular skiing lies on Barr Hill, behind the inn; the highest point of land is 2100 feet and the inn sits at 1650 feet elevation. The groomed and tracked trails are laid out to take advantage of the views and long downhills through the fields. At various times, one can see the three major mountains in this part of Vermont: Mansfield at Stowe, Jay Peak, and Burke.

The trails can be taken in short segments or long; most are designed for good intermediate skiers. There is opportunity for learners, too, because the Lodge keeps a staff of ski professionals to help. Long routes are available, including one north to the Craftsbury Sports Center and one south to Hardwick, 12 miles by road.

Each guest room is individually decorated, but this one takes the c with its fireplace, beam ceiling, period wallpape. and handmade quilt.

Left, the inn in the dead of winter, with unpicked fruit still on the tree.

THE INN ON THE COMMON

Perfect in every way

CRAFTSBURY COMMON is the quintessential Vermont village, and one of the most photographed in the state. It is not surprising to find an establishment there—the Inn on the Common—that embodies the perfect country inn.

This is an intimate inn. There are only four rooms in the main house, seven across the street in the south annex, and five around the corner in the north annex on the square. The south annex has a lavishly decorated common room and a small kitchen where guests can store food for lunches or snacks.

The main building at the Inn on the Common has a formal parlor and dining room exquisitely furnished with antiques and Oriental rugs—neatly proportioned rooms in a spacious old house. A former porch adjacent to the dining room, enclosed with floor-to-ceiling thermopane windows, with rattan furniture overlooks the rose garden.

The bedrooms exude comfort and style, enhanced by owner Penny Schmitt's ability to select just the right piece to show off each room's architectural advantage. She works constantly to perfect the décor, using only the best fabric and wallpaper, coordinating everything with custom-made drapes and spreads.

Guests are pampered with extra perks like turn-down chambermaid service at night, lush cotton terry bathrobes, Crabtree and Evelyn toilet products, and clock-radios.

Penny has worked with her staff to build a team of people who, in her words, "understand how important they are to the total effort." When guests gather in the library at the main inn for a before-dinner drink, an assistant manager serves as host, entertaining with tales of local history.

An unexpected delight is Michael's exceptional wine cellar. Many couples

Craftsbury Common is one of Vermont's most photographed villages. Its colonial heritage is exemplified by the 1820 Congregational Church facing the Common.

*Skiing to the nearby
ski center from the inn.*

return each year to sample it for additions to their own collections. He keeps on top of the market, so the wines are reasonably priced.

The menu for the evening is posted on a board in the dining room. The talented young chef, Yves Morrissette, comes out of the kitchen to explain the choices on the five-course menu. He is sold on the new, lighter cuisine and enjoys using his imagination in combining foods, but he is thoroughly grounded in classic technique from his training at the Culinary Institute of America.

The inn serves nothing but fresh ingredients, specializing in locally grown rabbit, fowl, pheasant, venison, lamb, and veal. Fresh seafood is available year-round and in summer, vegetables and herbs are picked from the inn's garden. Elegant china and crystal inspire guests to dress for dinner.

The inn has a AAA four-diamond rating; Penny believes this is the smallest inn in the U.S. to receive it, and she is sure it's the smallest in New England. She also has a risk-free, 800-number reservation service which guarantees return of deposit if no skiable snow.

SKIING AT THE INN ON THE COMMON

In February and March of 1791, Col. Ebenezer Crafts brought his family on sleds from Stockbridge, Massachusetts, to their new home, one of the first settlements in northeast Vermont. Residents cleared the common and shared the potato crop planted there. An early history comments, "Winters . . . clog the ability of its inhabitants for more than a third of the year."

Well, no more! The gentle terrain of lakes, river valley, and long meadows offers opportunities for play at the Craftsbury Nordic Ski Center, one of the most extensive systems in the East. Well marked trails groomed for skating and traditional techniques with new equipment can satisfy everyone from beginner to expert.

Inn guests can ski to the center or to the next village for lunch. Those who go to the center must purchase lunch tickets in the morning, because the number of

diners is limited. On weekends, there is shuttlebus service, although groups of ten or more can arrange for transport midweek.

Both short and long loops utilize the frozen surface of Big Hosmer Lake. One can go from a run on the lake to a handsome hardwood ridge for a round trip of about 18 kilometers. Next to the lake, a ridge dominated by mixed evergreens makes for some easy climbing and downhills. The level ground around the playing fields of the former prep school is a perfect teaching area.

There are 65 kilometers of groomed trails at the center and a total of 110 maintained in the area. Exchange tickets can be arranged with another center nearby.

Extensive backcountry trails can be reached via the system in the Lowell Range; guided tours are advised. The center has purchased 500 acres on Eden Mountain across the valley where it is developing trails; maps must be picked up at the office.

Early season training for competetive skiers.

*The lakeside view
of the inn.*

*Left, at breakfast, guests
come right into the kitchen
to collect hot dishes
that have been prepared
for them.*

FOLLANSBEE INN

Comfort above all

IF COMFORT could be packaged, it would come in a box labeled "Follansbee Inn." An air of relaxed ease, partly from surroundings that please the eye rather than overpower it, and partly from the laid-back style of innkeepers Sandy and Dick Reilein, are immediately apparent.

The inn is a prominent feature in this tiny village, with a Baptist Church built in 1794, a crossroads store and gas station, a post office, and a few houses that mark the center of what once was a bustling agricultural area. When city dwellers began seeking the countryside, one prosperous family whose farmhouse bordered Kezar Lake began enlarging their home to take in "summer boarders."

As time went on, it became a much-frequented roadside rest-stop. The tavern from those early days is the "fire room," whose Franklin stove, old beams, and low ceiling make it a cozy sitting room, and where ghosts cling in spite of any renovations.

Across the hall, with a view of the lake, is another sitting room with a small bar and fireplace. Sandy had an old wood stove chopped in half and topped with a pine slab to make a coffee table that doubles as a great conversation piece.

The Reileins serve dinner only to their inn guests, which adds to the intimacy, they feel. Sandy posts the menus on the chalkboard and treats it like a large dinner party. Dinner is served in the large room that faces the lake. The dining room has also been used successfully as a meeting room for hosting small groups and seminars.

A special Christmas weekend is held in early December, inviting guests to "step into the past." Guests enjoy a sleigh ride and Caroling Fest, a tour of six inns featuring seasonal decorations and holiday cookery, and the lighting

Dick and Sandy Reilein, now in their sixth year of innkeeping, and still smiling.

of the town Christmas tree. A map of the area's unique crafts shops is provided and it is also possible to cut a Christmas tree to take home.

Generally, however, guests entertain themselves. "You can never predict how a weekend will go when a group of strangers comes together," Sandy says. Breakfast usually gets things started. It is served buffet style, with juices, cereals, coffee, tea and fresh breads and rolls on a sideboard in the dining room. People wander in and out of the kitchen for their hot selections—omelets, hot cakes, waffles, whatever.

An inveterate antiques hound, Sandy turns the minutiae of life into marvelous decorative touches. It can be anything from a book or a posy to a child's dress on a doll in a bedroom. In the upstairs hallway she exhibits early cooking implements, on a full-size stove, including a chestnut cooker that only she could identify.

Son Matthew, a very self-possessed teenager, is now the assistant inn-keeper. Guests begin to feel part of the family, too; one Texas man arrives

bringing his own chili to share with the others.

SKIING AT
THE FOLLANSBEE INN

The Lake Sunapee region does not have mountains as high or lakes as large as the rest of New Hampshire, but neither does it have the over-development that

Meals are served family style.

84

Ready to go!

The Fire Room was the tavern in the old days of the inn—now it's a cozy sitting room.

has completely altered some resorts throughout the country. Instead, the area around New London, which offers guests entertainment, remains true to the atmosphere of the Follansbee Inn.

Both natural and commercial skiing areas are accessible directly from the inn. The trail around the lake leads to a low ridge on the opposite side with some challenging ups and downs, fine views, and a good picnic site. Behind the post office and general store in the village is a trail that follows a pine-covered ridge, opens onto old farm meadows, and eventually leads to the Norsk Ski Touring Center. This has 85 kilometers of groomed trails, and the Eastman Ski Touring Center, a short drive away, has another picturesque trail system, well marked and tracked.

In addition, there are golf courses and a number of trails on public land for which the Reileins can give directions. One can even ski to Georges Mill, the next town, by a combination of hiking trails and logging roads.

There is a good, three-mile walk around the lake; a neighbor down the road offers sleigh rides for a charge. Ice skating on the rink across the road is another option; and just sitting by the lake on a sunny afternoon can be followed by a cup of hot cider or kir back at the inn.

Downhillers can reserve tickets at King Ridge to speed their start in the morning. The mountain has a two-for-one mid-week rate and both the Ridge and Mount Sunapee have snowmaking.

For a change of pace, there are cultural events at the college, and shops and restaurants in New London.

MOOSE MOUNTAIN LODGE

Hosts who love skiing

THE BIG NEWS at Moose Mountain Lodge is that the moose are back! Absent for many years from northern New England, they are now permitted to walk anywhere they wish, including on cross country trails.

In spite of the information sent to guests in advance, nothing can quite prepare one for the inn's majestic location. Guests are treated to views of vast tracts of unspoiled countryside. It is possible to sit in the living room and gaze out over New Hampshire and **86** Vermont.

About the only distraction is to go skiing . . . or skating, or sliding, or to drive seven miles to Hanover for a quick injection of civilization from an Ivy League college town. That is where Dartmouth College conducts its annual Winter Carnival, the longest running observance of the rites of winter for the younger set.

Peter's father, Carl, was one of the pioneers of Eastern skiing and a founder of the Dartmouth Outing Club. It pleases Peter to be using some of the trails his father helped to build. Carl

*A very homey, woody,
loggy place.*

*A group of skiers
ready to go, led by
innkeeper Peter Shumway.
Ask him to tell you some stories of his
recent escapades
in the Alps. Tulla
the dog, a Weimaraner,
waits in anticipation.*

was a bit shocked when he learned how much Kay and Peter paid for the lodge back in 1975; he said they'd put up some pretty fine cabins in his day that cost no more than $100. Peter will be glad to point out one relic that's left on a trail.

Kay's family went to North Conway to ski in the thirties. Now she enjoys opening up her home to people like her who love to ski.

The Shumway's lodge was built from huge logs cut when the hillside was cleared for a downhill slope in 1938. The tow ran all the way to the bottom of the long hill (the inn lies at 1600 feet elevation), but only the fields around the inn are cleared now. Something of the devil-may-care spirit of the days of snow trains, wet woolens, and weekend parties clings to the lodge for anyone who remembers them. And there are still the homey rustic bed chambers to ensure sweet dreams.

Kay is always cooking up something special in the kitchen. She is happy to be serving healthier foods, and prepares more chicken, fish and pasta, and less **87**

red meats. There usually is one main offering at dinner, with choices in all that accompanies it. She is disappointed when guests decide to eat out. "They miss the most important part of the experience," she says, "the special feeling that develops when guests share a good meal."

The inn's policies are pretty relaxed. Evenings are sedate with Tulla, the Weimaraner, presiding before the fireplace in the main common room. Music drifting from the player piano in the game room downstairs may attract a few people for a little vocalizing. And if it's a clear night, Kay may even get everyone out for a moonlight ski.

SKIING AT MOOSE MOUNTAIN LODGE

The Shumways report that their guests are skiing more and better. Even without that incentive, Peter probably would go on expanding the trail system on their 350 acres because the family enjoys skiing so much. It's much more than a tradition for them.

One access trail climbs immediately behind the inn to a shoulder of South Peak. This has fairly challenging terrain and goes on to a long, wilderness trail that continues over North Peak to Lyme, about 20 kilometers away.

Skiers of more modest ability strike off from the inn along the access road to the beaver pond, where there is another connection with the higher trail or easier loops through fairly level hardwood growth. The Mink Brook Trail begins near the bottom of the road to the inn; a round trip would involve a good healthy climb, going out. Skiers can be shuttled to a Dartmouth Outing Club trail and take only the downhill return leg, a delightful tour with a brook for company part way.

The recently re-routed Appalachian Trail crosses on this side of South Peak; both old and new approaches can be reached through the inn trail system, but not all is skiable. There are miles of other logging and unplowed town roads, as well as the groomed center at Woodstock, Vermont, and at the Dartmouth Ski Touring Center.

Snowshoeing and skating on the pond are alternative choices.

Peter and Kay believe that breaking through fresh snow is the ultimate in cross country skiing.

GOLDEN EAGLE LODGE

A full-scale, four season destination resort

Mt. Tecumseh, in the background, presides over the best in both nordic and alpine skiing.

THE GOLDEN EAGLE LODGE at Waterville Valley is not an old-fashioned inn; it is a new-fashioned one, the flagship hotel for the company that has created a ski town to rival any in the country. Skier polls invariably give it high marks. And now, to meet demand, the Waterville Company has incorporated cross country facilities into its master plan.

Most of what is here is the brainchild of Tom Corcoran, former U.S. Olympic alpine competitor. After attending Harvard Business School, he spent several years in top-level management at Aspen, Colorado, during its expansion years in the early Sixties. When Ralph Bean pioneered a new development corporation in the Sixties, he chose Corcoran to head it. Waterville Valley is now a full-scale, four-season destination resort.

In addition to the indoor pool, whirlpools and sauna in the lodge, guests are entitled to use of all facilities at the Sports Center. They include a 25-meter pool; wading pool for children; steam rooms; racquet sports; fitness center; tanning booths; separate room with video games and table sports; and a running track. Tennis, aerobics classes and massage are available for a fee.

Parents like the economy of renting separate and complete living units, with maid service, fully outfitted for having meals in if they choose. There are other perks, too.

Children take to condominium living combined with hotel amenities faster than ducklings to water. They enjoy the freedom of going alone to the pool or to friends' rooms, or even down the hill to the Town Square.

There is the added convenience of the free shuttle bus. It makes a full circuit of the valley, including the base lodge at the alpine center, frequently throughout the day and evenings during holidays. In the evening there are sleigh rides and hockey games in the enclosed skating rink at the Town Square. Hours for free skating are scheduled daily.

Traditional, rustic spaces.

WATERVILLE VALLEY PHOTOS

The village is surrounded by cross country ski trails.

SKIING AT THE GOLDEN EAGLE LODGE

Mountains rise dramatically from the valley floor on all sides, affording both shelter and stunning scenery. Famed though the alpine facilities are, cross country skiers are scarcely underprivileged. Their services are located at the Town Square, and they can ski straight out around Corcoran's Pond to the network, 100 kilometers of trails, 70 kilometers groomed and tracked.

To the south and east, trails lie along a narrow valley on the lower slopes of Snow's Mountain and Jennings Peak. They fan out on both sides of Snow's Brook from a novice trail that runs the length of the valley, given different names along the way to distinguish the sections. On the north end of the valley lie even more novice and intermediate trails on land surrounding the Mad River.

On weekends, trail tickets are sold at the Snow's Mountain alpine center. Another intermediate trail circles it on a long climb to a height near the top of the alpine trails with a picnic table and views of the big mountain, Tecumseh, to the west. There is an expert loop along Cascade Brook and an unplowed road into backcountry hooks into it.

For a taste of the alpine scene, one can ride the bus to the base lodge, have lunch and ski back via the Pipeline to the village. Bull Hill Cabin at the center of the two networks on the east side of the valley offers light lunches and hot or cold beverages.

Full equipment rentals, gear and clothing, as well as certified instructors, can be found at the cross country center on the Square. The teaching area is just across the pond. The shop has pulks for rent, low sleds for pulling loads that are popular now for carrying children.

The Company looks kindly upon seniors, giving over-50s lower rates. There also are packaged lesson plans.

The Town Square is a collection of multi-level, Cape Cod style buildings erected around a horseshoe-shaped green, with a pond at its open end. Eating places range from classy lounges with entertainment to a fast food parlor to a charming small coffee house where one can have breakfast or snack after skiing. Shops offer everything from books to jewelry to T-shirts. A deli can take care of a quick lunch or last-minute items forgotten on the grocery list.

Innkeeper Mark Anderson is very much a presence and accessible to guests. There is 24-hour service at the desk, and coffee and tea are served in the morning and late afternoon in the two-story common room by the fireplace in the hotel lobby.

*An 1826 farmhouse
that is now an haute cuisine
inn set in New Hampshire's
Mount Washington Valley.*

THE DARBY FIELD INN

World-class scenery;
first class cooking

IT MIGHT be assumed that Darby Field Inn, at the entrance to the Mountain Washington Valley, is named for the clearing in which it sits . . . or a famous battlefield. Not so. Darby Field was an intrepid and some say slightly crazy Irishman who first climbed the mountain that dominates this New Hampshire landscape. The hardships he suffered are almost unimaginable.

The year was 1642, and the tiny settlements along the coast were barely established. Good old Darby even had to make the final part of the climb alone; his Indian guides feared the spirits who ruled the mountain. And yet after all that, he never did find the precious gems rumored to be found there. While sitting in the comfort of the inn that bears his name, one is overwhelmed by the awesome majesty of the land and its powerful beauty. While basking in the gracious hospitality of owners Marc and Maria Donaldson one might be forgiven a bit of self-congratulations for having discovered the inn.

The memorable cuisine is created by Marc, the head chef, who learned the restaurant business from a Japanese master chef who became a mentor and planted the idea for the inn. A stint as an executive chef in South America, where he met Maria, a journalist born in Spain, was followed by an extended visit to Japan. When the pair decided to settle down and get serious about having a family, the inn business seemed a natural.

Their cosmopolitan tastes reveal themselves in the dinner menus, which give Marc a chance to try unusual ways with flavors, herbs, and styles. He has

The fieldstone fireplace dominates the sitting room.

taken dishes from around the world and adapted them to American tastes.

Since they took over the inn in 1979, Marc and Maria have given tirelessly of themselves and their resources. The oldest part of the inn, an 1826 farmhouse, is filled with wrought iron chandeliers, stair railings, and other decorative trim made in the blacksmith shop that once operated on what is now the lower level. A fieldstone fireplace covering one wall of the living room competes in scale with the view of the Valley through the picture window.

Toward the front of the inn, the cocktail lounge is visible through a window wall adjoining the living room. This makes a convenient gathering place for outside dinner guests. A sunny nook opposite it has card tables and a piano.

The décor of each bedroom creates a unique personality, using windows, lighting, and antiques in an understated way. The most spectacular is a triangular-shaped bedroom with a queen-sized sleigh bed bearing a high, carved headboard.

Maria now devotes most of her time to the family, but the children are learning the business, too, and already know how to make guests feel at home. Son Jeremiah, for instance, can advise about ice fishing in Silver Lake.

Honeymooners from the forties returning recently reported the ambience was exactly the same and that the Donaldsons only had improved the inn.

SKIING AT THE DARBY FIELD INN

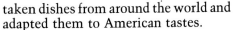

A low, wooded hill rises close behind the inn, providing shelter from the winds. A figure eight loop of modest degree lies in the woods along the lower part of the ridge, suitable for skiers of modest ability. For a more challenging excursion, one can climb to the top of the ridge from Tangent or encircle it.

The Creamery leads directly out from the inn along a sheltered gully to another network offering longer distances. These trails are on neighbors' lands and are groomed, but not always widely. After crossing a traveled road, there are two choices. The first and shorter route takes one down the opposite side of the ridge to a beaver pond and meadow where the terrain is more even.

Branching off this trail is a longer one called Kodiak, which climbs through a mature stand of hardwoods to high ground. There is a great picnic destination at an overlook facing south, where Route 16 winds through a quiet, narrow valley dotted with farms, quite unlike the resort mecca lying on the inn side.

The final approach to the overlook is steep and may require sidestepping down, depending on conditions. Most of the return trip is a downhill romp, welcome after the climb, but all of it worthwhile.

The inn actually is located about a stone's throw from the Kancamagus Highway, one of the most scenic drives in the East, through the White Mountain National Forest. There are any number of public trails; the Donaldsons can advise where to get maps.

Sleigh rides, sledding, skating, ice climbing, and commercial cross country centers can be found in the Valley.

96

Left, the dining room, where chef-innkeeper Marc Donaldson serves memorable cuisine from around the world that he has adapted to American tastes.

This is the low, wooded hill that rises behind the inn, and is suitable for average skiers.

Right, from the charming guest room you can see the front yard, where the trails begin.

97

THE NOTCHLAND INN

Victorian grandeur

IN 1832, Nathaniel Hawthorne called Crawford Notch "a great artery through which the lifeblood of international commerce is continually throbbing between Maine and the Green Mountains and the shores of the St. Lawrence." He described the throng of carriages, coaches, carts, and droves of cattle that lined up for the climb in summer; the building of the railroad through the Notch in 1861 only increased the traffic.

The pioneer Crawford family had the most famous hostelry, at the top of the Notch, and one son ran another on his farm farther down the mountain. At mid-century, an eccentric Boston millionaire named Samuel Bemis, who hiked into the Notch daily from North Conway, bought this farm and other land along the Saco River at Hart's Location, four miles from Bartlett and five from the head of the Notch.

In 1862, Bemis moved into his magnificent, newly built Victorian mansion, fashioned of granite and heavy timbers. The interiors match the impressive size and solidity of the architecture, with high ceilings and fireplaces in all of the 30 rooms.

The inn is noted for its five-course gourmet meals.

The big sleigh is pulled by Belgian draft horses. Below, the inn, built of granite and heavy timbers, with fireplaces in every room.

Guest accommodations consist of seven deluxe rooms and four suites, all with working fireplaces and private tiled baths. The rooms are individually decorated with matching Laura Ashley style quilts, drapes, and wall coverings that blend with the antique and traditional furnishings.

At the center of the house is a room designed around the turn of the century by Gustav Stickley. Mahogany three-quarter paneling is balanced by a wall of windows. Its low, Spanish-style fireplace is striking. The Bernardins call this the Map Room, for its decorations, and here guests gather for indoctrination from John in local history and the lore of the inn.

The main dining room is the former Crawford Tavern, the oldest, continually used inn building in the region. It has been beautifully restored, with windows on two long walls and light birch furniture. A back-to-back fireplace wall separates it from a smaller dining room and glass sun room overlooking the mountains.

Outdoors, in the front, are Pat's special love, 200 feet of gardens. In the rear is a beguiling scene: a small pond for skating, lighted at night, and a gazebo with hot tub.

Two snug rooms have been outfitted in the old schoolhouse next door. A fireplace, nooks and crannies, and sloped ceiling upstairs make it a charming hideaway. The exteriors of the dining room wing, the schoolhouse, and the barns are preserved in beige paint that matches the original.

The Bernardins have a collection of rare domestic sheep which, along with a matched team of Belgian horses, have become something of an attraction in the area.

Most famous of all are Pat's five-

Handmade quilts brighten the guest rooms.

bove, the trail
nch arrives
 sleigh.
ft, resting
 a trail along
e Saco River.

course gourmet dinners. Guests wait eagerly to find out the evening's choices, marveling at the nonchalant way she turns out one masterpiece after another. Fresh ingredients are the rule of the house, and in summer many come from her garden.

John and Pat concentrate on making their guests feel comfortable and give them a lot of attention. "We like our guests to treat this grand old house as they would that of a friend," says John.

SKIING AT
THE NOTCHLAND INN

There are only 850 acres of private land left in the Notch and the Bernardins own 450 of them. Their cross country trails lie in the Saco River Valley, one of the few areas wide enough to allow farming during the early settlement of the region. These are broad meadows now grown up to white birch, beech, and maples.

John installs wooden bridges for the widest river crossings; other slow-running areas freeze over. Traveling upriver, a series of loops parallel the river, affording spectacular views of the narrowing cliffs on each side.

The downriver section first explores a small island where the trail is wide enough to accommodate the big sleigh, built by John and a friend and pulled by the Belgians. Moonlight skiing is a specialty on this sheltered glade.

John uses state-of-the-art equipment to groom the 20 kilometers of novice and intermediate trails he has laid out. Longer trips can be taken into the Dry River Wilderness Area of the White Mountain National Forest. These trails lie above the valley floor.

Gourmet trail lunches are available on request. Pat sometimes prepares a hot lunch for group outings, which she brings out on a sled. The innkeepers sometimes lead guided tours.

Within driving distance are many commercial ski centers, both alpine and cross country.

*Chinese rugs, antique beds,
Victorian chairs and sofas,
old chests—the inn is a treasure
house of collectibles.*

*Left, the inn was designed
by the famous architect,
Stanford White, as a luxurious
residence.*

INN AT THORN HILL

Architecture by Stanford White; hospitality by Peter and Linda

THE WHOLE ADVENTURE of innkeeping began for Peter and Linda LaRose almost as a joke; she and a friend began teasing their husbands, who were very much caught up in the high-powered Washington executive scene, about the idea. Peter, a key player in the early success of MCI, asked the first time she mentioned it, "What's a country inn?" Linda admits they'd never even stayed in one.

An ad for a seminar on buying an inn was the determining factor. After attending it, Linda persuaded Peter to start looking. Once they saw the village of Jackson, and the Inn at Thorn Hill, the decision to change lifestyles was easy.

Designed by Stanford White as an elegant residence, the inn would be a distinguished presence in any setting. Sitting on a rise at the edge of Jackson, it speaks of solidity, comfort, elegance, and distinction. All of this is borne out by its interior.

Linda's initial task was to completely furnish all of the rooms. With the aid of an antiques dealer who became a close friend, she re-established the Victorian character and mood of the house. Oriental carpets, carved and canopied beds, and antique appointments are beautifully arranged in spacious bedrooms. Sloped ceilings in smaller rooms on the third floor give the chambers a snug feeling. There is always something to entice the eye, including the work of artists who hold workshops here.

The drawing room at the inn extends across the side of the house facing Mount Washington and Pinkham Notch. A piano with music stand nearby and a wedding dress modeled on a dressmaker's form establish a period feeling. An old-fashioned, fully-licensed pub next to the dining room is an attractive nook for guests to visit before dinner.

The carriage house has a country rustic look with themes in each bedroom with patchwork quilts and antiques. The large sitting room and fireplace here make it especially appealing to families and conference groups. The building overlooks the outdoor swimming pool and the stream that cuts across the property. Small country cottages nearby with antique furnishings offer a special kind of retreat for those who appreciate real privacy.

The dining room at the rear overlooks the brook and low, wooded hills; it has a fireplace for evening interest. The LaRoses accommodate outside diners, but limit the number by assigning guests to a preferred dinner time.

The chef, a New England "jack of all **103**

Thorn Hill is in the middle of 200 km of world-class skiing.

trades" whose special talent is cooking, prefers hearty regional foods; lobster pie is the favorite dish with guests, says Linda, along with regulars like poached salmon and roast duckling in season. Because the chef and the rest of the staff treat the inn as if it were home, they create an atmosphere of complete comfort.

SKIING AT THE
INN AT THORN HILL

Jackson has a cross country skiing network that is the envy of most of the eastern resorts. They are up to 60 trails in their numbering system. The Jackson Ski Touring Foundation, which operates **104** *the center and maintains the trails, now*

has almost 200 kilometers of world-class skiing. And the village lies high enough in Pinkham Notch to be sure of good snow supply.

The approaching skier can have it wild and woolly or gentle. It can come with instruction and guide or purely undiluted.

Novice skiers slide around the village and its resorts making calls for coffee break, luncheon, or afternoon tea. Thorn Hill guests can enter the trails right at the inn.

Two mountain streams churn through the village. Along the Wildcat, a trail crosses a golf course and a low, wooded ridge to connect with a loop around the Eagle Mountain House and valley fields. The approach trail is rated moderately difficult, but there is a black diamond trail for an alternate return.

Across the covered bridge at the entrance to the village lies the Ellis River

Trail. This is a pleasant climb with changing views of the river, sometimes benign, sometimes rugged, that can end with lunch at Dana Place. The inn will provide shuttle service so that skiers can make just the downhill leg or be picked up.

An interesting innovation is a cooperative effort by Black Mountain Alpine Center, the Ski Touring Foundation, and the Jack Frost Ski Shops for a learn-to-ski program called the Great Ski Option. It offers lessons, rentals and trail privileges on January mornings at the ski touring center, and on afternoons at Black Mountain, on the same midweek package.

The large sitting room in the coach house has a relaxed, rustic comfort.

PHILBROOK FARM INN

Wide ranging ski trails over 1,000 acres

Preparing for a day's skiing.

PHILBROOK FARM is believed to be the oldest inn in the United States operated by the same family at the same site. Not only is it listed on the National Register of Historic Places, it embodies the history of Shelburne, New Hampshire. A sense of continuity pervades the place, along with a serenity that comes with exposure to the unchanging beauty of this northeastern entrance to the Mount Washington Valley.

Innkeepers Connie Leger and Nancy Philbrook and Connie's children, Ann and Larry, are so nonchalant about their rich family history that probably few people realize how much has gone into keeping the farm going.

The intervale where Shelburne is located is perhaps a mile across at its widest point and ten or twelve east and west, at most; the Androscoggin River meanders through it.

Philbrook Farm, with 1000 acres, is one of two major landowners in the town; the other a timber company, has several thousand acres. When Harvey and Suzannah Philbrook moved from Bethel, Maine, in the 1850s, it took real perseverance to make a success of farming; the soil was good but the growing season short. It soon became apparent that tourists would be good for the economy and, in 1861, after enlarging the house, they opened the inn. Before the end of the century, following the arrival of the railroad, Shelburne boasted six hotels.

Exactly 100 years after the original farmhouse was built, on a July afternoon in 1934 when the inn was full, the big attached barn burned to the ground. Shelburne townfolk turned out in force and moved every piece of furniture and personal belongings out of the inn. Once the fire was out and the danger over, they put it all back in place; guests sat down to dinner as if nothing had happened and slept in their own beds that night.

It would take a lot of visits to hear all the stories that Connie and Nancy have to tell—about their youth, all the family lore, the changes in the business. "The fun of it," says Nancy, "is seeing people come back, getting to know

The inn sits on 1000 acres of farmland at the entrance to Mount Washington Valley.

CLAIRE J. BERGERON PHOTO

whole families." She scoffs at the transient style of summer travel, when people don't really see much of the places they visit.

There is nothing old-fashioned about the service and the cuisine, except that chef Ann continues to offer good New England country fare, with her own flourishes. Nancy keeps her hand in making the pastries and the breads. Larry handles the business end. Connie turns out handcrafts that enliven the rooms. They all share in the general operation . . . and problems . . . along with a staff that stays for generations. One even had a room named after her.

SKIING AT PHILBROOK FARM INN

There's been skiing at Philbrook Farm since ladies wore long skirts and used wide, ten-foot skis and one "stick." The Nansen Ski Club at Berlin is the oldest ski club in the country, and Connie and Nancy remember going to ski dances held at nearby Gorham, its twin city, when they were girls. They skied on trails at Mt. Cranmore before the tramway was constructed; when the system was dismantled recently, they bought one of the old cars and set it up on the front lawn.

It was an easy matter to convert their logging roads and hiking trails when guests began looking for cross country skiing. All they had to do was add appropriate signs.

The trails begin on a shelf of land behind the inn where their cottages are hidden away. In one direction lies a broad plateau with old growth timber being harvested selectively. The trails are wide and good for snowshoeing, too.

About two kilometers to the west, the Philbrook Farm trail intersects the Appalachian Mountain Club's Millbrook Trail, the route the Appalachian Trail

takes into the Mahoosuc Range. This is for strong skiers using mountain skis only.

Going the other way from the inn, the trails are narrow and steep in places, climbing a long ridge to a peak with views of the intervale to the south and of the wild, rugged Mahoosucs to the north. Long traverses through the woods, zigzagging away from the trail, are neces-

Looking over the Intervale and the Androscoggin River, with Mount Washington's white peak in the background.

sary, or taking off one's skis, on parts of the return trip.

Not far away is the Evans Notch Road, unplowed in winter, which has a number of lumber roads and trails leading from it, all untracked skiing. A similar unused town road beginning in the village follows the river upstream.

On the highway to Gorham through the famous Shelburne birches, preserved by the town as a memorial to their war dead, a dam in the river created by the causeway for the railroad is a lovely spot for skating. The view of the Presidentials is spectacular.

Further afield in Pinkham Notch are marked AMC trails, as well as a small network maintained by the Nansen Ski Club in Berlin. There are commercial centers also in nearby Bethel, Maine.

PAUL AVIS PHOTO

THE BALSAMS / WILDERNESS

A ski resort with every amenity

DRIVING THROUGH Dixville Notch makes one appreciate what an undertaking it was in "the good old days" to take a vacation in the rugged New Hampshire mountains. The Balsams is located in one of the most celebrated scenic spots in New England.

At every turn in this grand old hotel there is visible proof of its appeal to 19th century travelers—old photos, period prints and cartoons, souvenirs and letters preserved under glass. Modernized though it has been, with every convenience, the spirit of those days clings to the place.

The inn's hallmark is the personal attention and service that guests receive ... indeed, coddling would be a better word. A pint of complimentary maple syrup awaits returning guests. Everyone receives a copy of USA Today, which shows up each morning at the door. There is a full calendar of activities from warm-up exercises before breakfast to moonlight sleigh rides.

Once here, everything is at hand; it is truly a destination resort. In spite of its size, the seclusion and the wild, rugged beauty of its setting contrive to make it seem a sheltered haven, cozy as a small inn.

Nightly excursions to the dining room reveal that the food is indeed a memorable highlight.

Executive Chef Phil Learned and his staff preside at a table where all choices are displayed. Buffet nights are legendary—Medieval banquets come to mind.

The dining room has recently been refurbished. It is a high-ceilinged, T-shaped room with half-pedestal columns. Although winter dress is more casual, the festivity inspires dressing up.

The pool and billiards parlor has four

The grand old 19th-cent hotel is a destination resort where there are plenty of things to do.

Dual tracked trails around Lake Gloriette.

*The Billiards Room
has plenty of tables.*

tables; the library, a quiet, enclosed verandah for reading; the capacious lounge, a grand piano, and a fireplace nook around the corner. On the entry level are two cocktail lounges with piano bar and live entertainment. The movie theater doubles as lecture hall and chapel for church services. Upstairs there is a large nightclub.

In an establishment where the employees outnumber the guests, it's a neat trick to keep all this running smoothly. The old pros who do so are Steve Barba and Warren Pearson who operate out of a glass-enclosed office right off the lobby. Steve began as a caddy at 13 and Warren came to run

the ski school in 1966 after serving in Vietnam.

Changing travel patterns and an aging clientele put the hotel in decline in the sixties. The citizens of nearby Colebrook persuaded a native son to buy it in 1954; in 1971 he asked Steve and Warren to run it. They not only turned the place around, but now own it with Chef Learned and another partner. They are proud that eighty percent of their business is repeat visits.

SKIING AT
THE BALSAMS

Cross country skiers are now the favored children at The Balsams. Their services are centered right at the hotel, in the ground level main entrance. They can buy or rent gear or have their skis waxed or meet their instructor and head out.

One can still ride the free shuttlebus to the hotel's alpine center across the valley. The practice hill is there, as well as beginner and intermediate trails that swing around the base of the mountain.

Most of the trails lie on the north side of Route 26 where the hotel sits. Beginner trails are laid out around Lake Gloriette and the nine-hole, executive golf course.

An intermediate loop leads around the lake to the alpine center or west along

the highway for a short distance before dipping into a pleasant shallow valley around Moose Brook. Advanced trails wind from here around the long ridge on which the golf course is built. A log shelter at 1600 feet is about midway on a 5.4 kilometer trail called Fox Trot, which also can be reached from the top.

To the north, intermediate trails begin directly behind the hotel or midway up the golf course road, a long, gradual climb of about 3 kilometers, rated novice. From the 2050-foot elevation, there is a panoramic view of the Upper Connecticut River Valley.

Between Mount Abeniki and Keyser Mountain, one can climb to Mud Pond, at 2272 feet, which is part of the inn's water supply system. A novice trail runs along the canal, where pine and spruce enclose it much of the way, and circles the pond. Guided picnic tours are brought here, with lunch delivered by the trail crew; a warming cabin is being built. An alternate trail leads back to the golf course road.

Some skiers cross over into alpine to strengthen their nordic skills, Warren observes; the hotel offers three free alpine or cross country lessons with a Ski Week stay. Topnotch professional instructors will teach latest techniques in both disciplines, including wilderness and telemark skiing.

KURT BROWN PHOTOS

*Left, the Gibson
Room makes a welcome
refuge on cold days,
with its glowing
fire and English
wing chairs.*

114

THE BETHEL INN & COUNTRY CLUB

An old beauty brought back to life

THE VERY CHARM of Bethel, Maine, its seeming isolation from the world, was almost its undoing as a resort. Built in 1913, the Bethel Inn was an elegant retreat for the patients of Dr. John George Gehring, whose success in treating those suffering from "nervous fatigue and exhaustion" won him the support of wealthy patrons willing to underwrite suitable accommodations for his clients and their guests.

One of those patients became the principal benefactor of the town and set up the corporation that controlled the inn until the doctor's death in the 1950s. By this time, many Americans were jetting to Europe or following the trend to seaside locations. The inn guests, who had the same rooms for so many years that their names were attached to them, were declining in all respects.

The inn's fortunes swung up and down with changes in ownership and management until the late seventies, when it was acquired by Richard Rasor and his Bethel Commodore Corporation. There was scarcely smooth sailing ahead. The second gas crisis in 1979 was followed by two years of no snow.

But Maine people had weathered hard times before. The community had a sound economic base: small manufacturing built on the logging industry; Gould Academy, one of New England's

The main inn building, whose snow-covered grounds provide good skiing for novices.

A light and airy guest room, delicately color coordinated, provides a restful respite from the ski trails.

115

toniest boarding schools; good small cross country and downhill centers; and the lakes and mountains that kept travelers re-discovering the back country.

When this high-powered former advertising executive hit town, there was concern about what changes might occur in the "grand old lady" on the town square. But Dick Rasor was just as concerned about retaining the best of the traditional inn while bringing the resort into modern times.

Long-time guests find the rooms just as they have always been, except refurbished; floral and calico prints in bedroom quilts and curtains; flowers and fireplaces. Graceful columns and sculptured paneling frame a classical pianist at the Steinway during dinner. Breakfast by a sunny window on the enclosed verandah overlooking the first tee of the golf course starts the day.

Business executives can combine meetings with an afternoon of skiing. Families can economize in one of the condominiums, where the only disturbance on the wide vista of the White and Mahoosuc mountains will be skiers sliding by on the cross country trails. The inn has lodgings in several cottages, as well.

The menu matches the size of the enormous dining room, a bountiful selection at every stage of a five-course meal. Continental cuisine and traditional New England fare are evenly balanced.

Inside, the level of innkeeping service continues the reputation of earlier days. Outdoors, a slight change of pace reflects the changes that have taken place. Otherwise, the grand old lady is still a fitting presence to the traditional green, with its mix of architectural styles that has qualified it for the National Register of Historic Places.

SKIING AT
THE BETHEL INN

When Dick Rasor was looking for a business to invest in, he didn't much care where it was located, as long as it had skiing on one side of the property and golf on the other. Bethel had both, and the town has benefitted from another entrepreneur with the same kind of long-term, personal commitment that has turned the Sunday River alpine and cross country centers into leaders in their field.

In the early 1900s and 1920s, Bethel Inn guests enjoyed skiing and skating, plus a long, wooden toboggan slide on the gentle slope now occupied by the golf

Left, cross country skiers leaving the inn on a trek over the 28 km of groomed trails.

Skiers nearing the end of the three mile trip to the inn's Lake House.

course. Winter sports didn't justify a fourth travel season until the last decade, however.

Broad, double-tracked courses are laid out on the 18-hole course in loops that only occasionally circle in sight of each other. The long ridge loses itself in adjacent woodlands where the terrain tightens up a bit and develops a decided tilt along the lower side. Most of the trails are rated moderate skiing. Longer tours hook in on Balsam Run and I-95, a former logging road that also leads to mostly level skiing.

In addition to Sunday River, Mt. Abrams Alpine Center is only minutes away; Wildcat Mountain and the Balsams are longer drives. Several commercial cross country centers can be found, and scads of trails lie on National Forest lands.

Sally Sawyer and Leslie Kavanagh are PSIA-qualified instructors who take care of the ski shop in the inn. They also sign up guests for sleigh rides, pulled by a team of big Belgian horses, and for moonlight ski tours.

A plus for anyone who buys a day-use ticket is full access to the inn's recreation center, equipped with heated, indoor-outdoor swimming pool, sauna, Jacuzzi, gym and game room.

117

SUNDAY RIVER INN AND CROSS COUNTRY SKI CENTER

A ski touring center where everybody has a good time

STEVE WIGHT has been taking a lot of kidding from his long-time friends in the cross country ski business lately. For years he resisted signs that the sport might be succumbing to the glitz that had overtaken the downhillers. But when he showed up at a ski area operators meeting wearing a Lycra suit, everybody knew the revolution had come!

An Elderhostel group lives it up.

Now, it was not by slim, young things whipping out to show off their techniques that Steve's mind was turned. It was from observing his older guests, particularly the Elderhostel groups. What Steve realized was that people are coming to skiing on skinny boards in the same way they do to downhill. They want to have Fun! No more socks and jeans and slogging around the best way possible. Pursuing another vision of oneself is part of the fun, and if a sharp outfit contributes to that sense of participating fully in the sport, Steve is all for it.

Sun deck at the ski shop, below, and the ski shop interior, left, with lots of things to buy.

Nor is this a frivolous thing, he insists. More people are taking instruction, too. They want to learn to ski well *and* look the part.

Canadian "Canoe Chair" and table.

Sunday River Inn was the first commercial operation in the country to host the Elderhostel program and conducts seventeen a year, including six centered on downhill and three on cross country skiing.

The inn is particularly well suited to handling groups and is regularly sought by families for reunions and by church groups. Appalachian Mountain Club members frequently make it a headquarters, too. The most recent addition is a large room suitable for lectures and movies that connects the inn's main common room with the ski shop.

A special feeling of camaraderie permeates the inn, created by a pleasant **119**

Step out the door and start skiing.

combination of Steve and his wife Peggy's informality, the buffet-style serving for meals, and even the dormitory bathrooms.

During the day, everyone goes his or her own way. The social hour before dinner, to which guests can bring their own liquid cheer, is a real tradition. Steve and Peggy keep an eye on the process to be sure there are no wallflowers. The fieldstone fireplace works its magic, and the conversation is lively.

After dinner, the mood is quieter; books and reading matter are brought out; the game tables and perpetual jigsaw puzzle get a workout; a few people gather around the single TV set. A large game room in the basement gives young people a place to retreat.

Every time the front door opens during the day, wonderful odors drift out from the kitchen through the archway over the serving counter. Grown men can be seen wandering by like kids checking on the goodies coming out of the oven.

The L-shaped dining area is bright with windows, revealing handmade furniture fashioned from pine and birch. The tables have bases made from gear drives, designed by a craftsman friend of the Wights.

SKIING AT SUNDAY RIVER INN

Farming and lumbering made the Androscoggin Valley prosperous in early days, and the trail names at the Sunday River Inn and Cross Country Ski Center

commemorate them. Two-sled, Jill Poke, Tote Team, and Cruiser explore the ridge that climbs toward the Sunday River alpine center. Hardwood and pine grow in broad bands across the ridge, and the grade makes for some great downhill swoops.

In the woods close by the inn are several interconnecting trails, including American Harrow, Brown Jug, and Cant Dog, designed for skiers of modest ability, who can adjust the time out to their stamina. A picturesque trail is Wanigan, with an ideal mix of up, down, and level. This is also an alternative route to the Covered Bridge Trail; its destination is one of the most photographed of Maine's bridges, good for a picnic stop.

The Cross Country Center has classes both morning and afternoon with certified instructors, and more on weekends as demand calls for it. Except for the upper trails, most of the system is double-tracked and groomed for skating. Local schools are given the opportunity to bring their youngsters for instruction, and the ski team trains here, with help from the pro staff.

Sunday River also has some just-for-fun events for real Sunday skiers. The big one is a race at the end of March that closes out the season—the Pole, Paddle, and Paw is a ski, canoe, and snowshoe affair that can turn into almost anything depending on spring conditions.

Sunday River's alpine trails can be seen in the background of this photograph showing cross country trails.

Ski trails dotted with park benches for the weary are the ultimate in luxury.

The inn glows warmly at Christmas time.

Left, the dining room, formerly the parlor.

THE INN ON WINTER'S HILL

The legacy of famous brothers brought to life by corporate dropouts

IN 1895, this mansion was the talk of the town. Amos Winter built it to woo his wife Julia, setting it by itself on a hill, a jewel overlooking the Carrabassett Valley and the mountains surrounding it.

Amos asked his friends, the Stanley brothers, who had patented photo-processing equipment, to design his house. Favoring the Georgian Revival style, they put their stamp on a number of fine old buildings that still add class and character to Kingfield.

The Winter home was the first in Maine to have central heating. It was supplied by the original steam boiler from a narrow-gauge locomotive, which still anchors the house. (Half the building would have to come out to remove it.) Two years later, F. E. Stanley invented the Stanley Steamer that made transportation history. There may well have been a direct connection.

This house had everything: a soaring arch and fanlight over the front door; a music room with a box grand piano; a "front parlor" and dining room; a wide foyer and sweeping staircase with ram's horn newels. Upstairs, was yet another sitting room surrounded by four luxurious bedrooms. Some rooms had fireplaces and all had fashionable, pressed tin ceilings.

No one would know, looking at the carefully tended Victorian interior and furnishings today, that the mansion had known hard times. But for several years after Amos, III, sold it in 1953, the lower level was converted into a professional office. Among other things, linoleum covered the hardwood floors.

SUSAN G. DRINKER PHOTO

The sweeping Grand Stairway attests to the quality of the recent restoration by the present innkeepers.

One other owner ran it as an inn before Richard Winnick, his sister Diane, and partner Carolyn Rainaud discovered it a few years ago. They have poured themselves and a lot of money into restoring it. Gleaming floors and woodwork in maple, birch, cherry, and oak are only part of the testimony to their efforts.

The partners gained a wing of modern rooms with TVs and telephones in a **123**

The inn sits on a hill and provides wonderful views from the guest rooms.

SKIING AT THE INN ON WINTER'S HILL

The West Branch River snuggles up to the inn's six-acre hilltop, which is rimmed by pine and apple trees. Endless miles of marked snowmobile trails crisscross the Carrabasset Valley, beginning here.

A pleasant route for novice skiers encircles the town, breaking away in new directions if desired or turning back into it. One can have lunch at a restaurant, visit the Stanley Museum in the school building designed by the famous brothers, or delve into the town's past at the local historical museum. Kingfield, named for Maine's first governor (also a native son).

Decades after the last Amos Winter began cutting trails for skiing on Sugarloaf, it has moved into the top ranks as an alpine center. Near the base of the mountain is Maine's largest cross country area, the Carrabassett Valley Ski Touring Center.

It has 85 kilometers of groomed trails for both classic and skating techniques, and a full schedule of races and special events are held under the guidance of

restored connected barn, and covered its exterior in Queen Anne shingling to blend with the main house. Linking the two is an earlier addition, serving as a playroom, with video games and pool table, and a lounge, where light snacks, suppers, and drinks are served. A Palladian window and skylight make this a most compelling space.

The former parlor is the main dining room and the original family dining room is now called the breakfast room. It has grand views of Mount Abraham and Sugarloaf Mountain.

Richard and Carolyn share chef's honors, admitting that they enjoy experimenting with new combinations. They guarantee a "fine dining experience" with their delicious seven-course dinners, and a selection to match any palate. Special wine-tasting dinners are offered throughout the year.

Admitted corporate dropouts, the three traveled widely to gather ideas before settling into the inn business. They are justifiably proud to have been selected recently as a Carriage House **124** Inn by Clarion Hotels International.

A team of snow-white Siberian Huskies pulls the dog sled, a popular ride with guests.

Steve Davis. Teaching space for novices, loops for intermediate skiers, and challenging trails for experts that climb the mountainside are interspersed here.

A lodge with complete services in a lovely wilderness setting provides the right send-off. The community skating rink is located here, too, open to the public at stated times. Shuttle bus service covers this and the alpine center from town.

Access to public trails can be found for backcountry exploration. Intrepid trekkers can ski back to Kingfield on an intermediate trail of more than 20 kilometers that connects with civilization along the way.

Left, the perfect end to a perfect day.

125

LITTLE LYFORD POND CAMPS

Roughing it in the wilderness pays great skiing dividends

KATE spotted the for sale advertisement in *Yankee* magazine. It wasn't time to think about retirement for Bud, but she was intrigued. Little Lyford Pond Camps sounded like just the sort of place they'd always looked for on their own trips— a wilderness lodge, located in the Moosehead Lake region of Maine that offered hiking, fishing and cross country skiing vacations. Before the year was out, they owned it.

That was 1987, and the Fackelmans are sure now they have the best of all possible worlds. They share the duties at the lodge and Bud can continue his work on a flexible, part-time schedule, commuting by snowmobile, auto, and plane as necessary. He is a professor of veterinary surgery at Tufts University and a professor of animal and veterinary sciences at the University of Maine.

In the beginning, friends asked, "What are you going to do up there in the long, cold, lonely winters?" "Since we are in the cross country ski business," says Kate, "the longer and colder the winter, the better off we are." As for being lonely, they entertain people all winter who want to have just a small piece of the solitude and serenity that the Fackelmans enjoy all year.

It takes a bit of planning to get there.

Rustic cabins in a wilderness setting.

Taxi!

Solitude.

The most direct way is to hire Folsom's Flying Service at Greenville and land by ski plane on a pond near the camp. Folsom's is also the radio link between the Fackelmans and the outside world when confirming arrivals.

Alternatively, one can drive to an area where parking is permitted by the paper company that owns the land surrounding the camp. From there, one can ski in about eight kilometers. Gear can be picked up and delivered by snowmobile, but by either route, a small pack is suggested.

Life is very simple for guests. The Fackelmans have all the hard work. Individual log cabins become private retreats. Each has its own woodstove, propane gas lamps, cold running water, enameled basins for washing, beds

127

Ready for the trail.

made of pine logs, and a rocking chair. The sweet smell of pine wood fills the room.

Most guests use the sauna at the end of the day for the bathing ritual. A pail of water for each person is set by the stove in the kitchen late in the afternoon and everyone works out a schedule for time in the "oven."

Meals are served in the main lodge, where guests gather in the evening to socialize, read, or play checkers. Both Kate and Bud love to cook, leaning to "good old American food." They make their own breads and do a fair amount of vegetarian cooking, as Kate says, "even when we don't have vegetarians here." She is big on salads. They do need to know specific dietary requests in advance, because they can't run down to the supermarket. Box lunches are distributed every morning.

It takes careful logistical planning to sustain this winter operation. The Fackelmans begin in the fall to stock up on supplies, fill the root cellar and stack up wood for the cabins. They do have a generator, which is run a couple of hours a day for essentials like the water pump, washing machine and battery charging.

SKIING AT LITTLE LYFORD POND CAMPS

128 *A lot of people don't know what "back*

country" means, Kate warns, and come only to find that the skiing is a lot more rigorous than they expected. Says this former suburban Boston faculty wife, "They find that six miles at Little Lyford is a lot 'longer' than six miles on the Newton golf course. The trails are well marked and cleared (unless we have had a very recent wind storm), but they are not groomed or even necessarily tracked. We don't have benches on which to rest, nor warming huts along the way. We do have spectacular scenery, a lot of natural beauty, and tranquility."

Four mountains—Indian, Baker, Elephant, and Whitecap—contribute to the "spectacular" part. There are trails to ponds that lie at their feet and a few that climb them. The most popular has always been the trip along the Pleasant River to Gulf Hagas gorge, called Maine's Grand Canyon.

The current route from the Katahdin Iron Works road to the camps follows a trail up the broad valley of the West Branch of the Pleasant River. It begins at 700 feet elevation at the base of Chairback Mountain and climbs very gradually to 1216 feet at the camps. The Appalachian Trail passes near here on the way to Katahdin.

Wild game and birds create brief diversions; otherwise it's solitude, scenery, and bracing, clean air, among the rarest commodities in modern American life. Anyone who has stayed at Little Lyford will back the Fackelmans' claim that they can offer the best backcountry skiing experience in the East.

Preparing to return to the real world— on skis.

Each cabin has its own private privy.

View from Iceberg Mountain in the Laurentians.

QUEBEC

Dog sledding on
Lake Massawippi
in front of the inn.

Left, eating is
one of the main
activities to look
forward to at
Hovey Manor.

HOVEY MANOR

A 5 "fleur-de lis" inn

THE GENTLY ROLLING country-side around Lake Massawippi was a welcoming sight to the British loyalists leaving New England during the Revolution, among them Col. Ebenezer Hovey, for whom the Manor is named. Later came wealthy southerners, following the Civil War, who refused to return to their former vacation spots in "Yankeeland." By the 1890s, they were building handsome summer homes. Many of the families still hold these and come year-round, and the area remains a pocket where "Anglos" can feel at home.

The most splendid mansion on the western shore was "The Birches," now the Manor, built in 1900 by Henry Atkinson, owner of Georgia Power in Atlanta, who replicated George Washington's Mount Vernon, with its broad verandahs and white pillars.

During the thirteen years Stephen and Kathryn Stafford have owned the inn, they have done a marvelous job of improving and modernizing while still maintaining the integrity of the buildings. The former servants' quarters, ice house, pump and electric houses, and caretaker's residence have been converted into attractive lodgings. For a relaxing *après-ski* atmosphere, there is the historic Coach House Bar, which has an immense fireplace and is filled with Indian artifacts and farm antiques.

Much of the antique furniture is original to the home. Each bedroom is individually appointed, some with canopy beds and handpainted furniture, many with fireplaces, Jacuzzis, and balconies. Fine fabrics in curtains and spreads, and rich textures in wallpaper adorn spacious rooms. In the small bar next to the dining room hangs an unusual portrait of George Washington, which according to Steve was painted by "a dilettante from Philadelphia."

Almost a full wall of the living room

The fireplace alcove in the dining room.

133

is given to a fieldstone fireplace with full-length bookcases filling the opposite wall. The mahogany paneling is highlighted by the bold reds and greens that dominate the cushion coverings and draperies. French doors lead to a verandah overlooking the lake.

The fireplace alcove in the dining room might be found in any early Colonial home. Heavy beams overhead and knotty pine woodwork are balanced by spindle-backed chairs and small tables. On weekends, a classical pianist entertains at the grand piano placed near the entrance. "Good casual" is the way Steve describes the dress code; the atmosphere as a whole is friendly and informal, but he requests "no jeans and no boots."

The Manor is known for one of the finest contemporary French restaurants in the Province. For years it has received the highest rating for cuisine, four "forks," from the Quebec Ministry of Tourism. This, combined with its five "fleur-de-lis" rating for comfort and service, puts Hovey Manor among the top few country recreational retreats in all of Quebec. Six times a year, Steve presents special gourmet dinner parties, featuring seven original courses, each accompanied by a select wine. On any evening, however, five and six course "discovery" menus are available.

Snow-covered conifers make any cross country trail attractive.

SKIING AT HOVEY MANOR

Many guests are happy to slide around on the lake which also has a skating rink. A modest round of trails can be reached via the driveway on the hill behind the inn. They continue on into the village, where there are shops and restaurants.

A long trail called Skiwippi is maintained along the west shore by Hovey Manor and two other inns, which together offer a touring package. Steve recommends making the 12-kilometer trip from Les Sommets, the summit, back to the inn. This part of the trail has a net descent of 700 to 800 feet. If anyone tires and wants to stop, Katevale, a small cross country center, is located a short distance from its beginning. The inn does provide pick-up service.

The full run is challenging and fun. The first ridge is covered with conifers, where the trail tends to be narrow and choppy. A mid-section of meadows and open space near habitation is followed by a stiff climb to another high, wooded ridge. The longest section winds up and down through big hardwoods that give occasional glimpses of the lake before

Right, the inn and guest rooms are finely furnished with antiques and furniture original to the house.

Left, the newly decorated living room.

breaking out into fields not far from the inn.

The Skiwippi trail is marked and groomed but should be considered woods skiing. For wide, double-tracked trails there is Mt. Orford Provincial Park, twenty minutes away by car.

Fishing lunches, an innovation this year, take advantage of one of the chef's love of ice fishing and his familiarity with the lake. The day's catch is cooked fresh, and eaten with accompaniments, in a deluxe fishing cabin erected on the ice that has windows, woodstove, and a narrow deck. It's a bit like a small houseboat that sails nowhere; guests do the fishing, of course.

AUBERGE HANDFIELD

Premier dining with riverside ambience

Major attention is paid to food at Handfield, where continental and new French Canadian cuisine are popular.

THE VALLEY of the Richelieu River, which flows north from Lake Champlain to the St. Lawrence, is often called Quebec's garden district—a pleasant, lush region of farms and historic sites. The region also is defined by a series of low mountains that, lying south and east of Montreal, give it its name, Monteregie.

The Auberge Handfield hugs the shoreline of the Richelieu at the edge of Saint-Marc-sur-Richelieu, a typical, small village. Three generations have devoted their energies to developing their patrimony, and the inn is the most modern extension of the family farm, which is still being operated here.

Conrad Handfield and his mother opened their home to summer visitors in 1945, taking advantage of their riverside location and attracting guests with the bountiful food for which they became famous. In 1966, they began staying open year-round, and in each decade since, they have expanded their offerings.

Dining facilities predominate at the inn. The central room has a large fieldstone fireplace and extensions on the front and side expand the views of the river and lawns. These rooms surround the living room, which has its original fireplace and family mementos. It is brightened by the solarium built at one end of the porch-dining room.

On the river side of the highway, a series of low cottages are well spaced to preserve the views. In recent, mild winters, the broad stream has not frozen, and river gazing could be included in the indoor winter activities. When it does freeze, there is skating from the village to the auberge.

A modern building recently was added that combines facilities for boat travelers renting space at the marina in

One of the 200-year-old houses recently restored for lodgings, with hand-hewn log walls and beamed ceilings.

137

summer with those of a health salon. Licensed professionals administer the most up-to-date hydrotherapy, massage, and beauty treatments.

Several houses more than 200 years old have been moved to the inn property and restored for lodgings, retaining the hewn beams and wood interiors. All the bedrooms are decorated with handmade furniture typical of the region, but equipped with modern tile baths and TV sets.

The buildings are unified in their distinctive white stucco exteriors, a characteristic Quebec style of covering log houses in an earlier time, set off by a light blue trim. Together they form a small village of their own.

The excellence of the continental and new French Canadian cuisine can be judged by the inn's popularity with Montrealers. The Sunday buffet is especially favored, but every meal brings wide-ranging choices.

The Handfields operate one of the largest sugarhouses in the area, the *cabane a sucre*. Going out into the countryside during the sugaring season, March and April, is an important rite of spring for Canadians. The Handfield *cabane* can serve 150 people at a time in two long halls attached to the former barn where the huge evaporating machine is set up to boil the maple sap.

SKIING AT AUBERGE HANDFIELD

A beginner's trail of six to seven kilometers, described as a "ramble," through the fields and woods of the family farm is accessible from the back lawn of the inn. Special trails lead on to the cabane a sucre, *about 16 kilometers away, where a fire, drinks, and snacks are available.*

During the sugaring season, a full kitchen operation goes on throughout the day, serving famous Quebec specialties like Grand-Pères, *dough cooked in syrup; everything from eggs to meat given the sweet treatment; and of course traditional pea soup and baked beans. Early in the winter, one has to settle for roaming the paths through the woods here.*

There are two cross country centers within a few minutes drive of the inn. The provincial park at Mont-Saint-Bruno, located toward Montreal on the autoroute, has 30 kilometers of prepared trails. There are a nature interpretive center and shelters with toilet facilities, but no services. At least one easy trail goes to a lookout and one to a small lake. Most of the trails are in the medium difficulty range and encircle other lakes lying on this low peak. One difficult trail climbs to its height, about 1500 feet.

Beloeil is a small city with some handsome old houses and art galleries. Across the river from it on a low mountain at the edge of the residential district, McGill University has a nature center and observatory with hiking trails open to skiers in winter. This is a heavily wooded area, but there are occasional vistas.

Upstream from the inn there is a small island to explore, and sleigh rides are held on the grounds. One special note: Conrad has a great story about the ferry boat he converted to a summer theater.

Furnishings throughout the inn are eclectic, but blend together harmoniously, as in the reading lounge, above, and guest room, below.

138

The ski shop at Le Chantecler serves both nordic and alpine skiers, who can also relax on the sun deck over the shop.

Right, guests relax in conversation in front of the fireplace in the main lounge.

HÔTEL LE CHANTECLER

A magnet for skiers in the Laurentians

ALWAYS one of the foremost resorts in the Laurentians, Le Chantecler does not dwell on its past. Those remembering its early days—when a ski lift was set up on the hill next to the inn, and rooms added over the curling rink in its first expansion—will be amazed at its transformation.

In winter, skiing is king at Le Chantecler. The rooster, the symbol of the hotel, taken from a legendary figure in an Edmond Rostand play, has been adapted to signify "the Crest of the Laurentians," the peak of excitement and challenge in the alpine network that now extends westward over four mountains. Several million dollars have gone into bringing the hotel back from troubled times.

Flanking the heart of the hotel, a new wing steps down in tiers toward the lake, taking advantage of lake and mountain views. And condominium apartments stretch up the hill behind this core.

Entering the reception area, eyes are immediately drawn to the French doors, to the high windows and beyond, to the fieldstone terrace that is one of the hotel's signatures. Rivaling the finest alpine sunning spots, without having to ride the lifts, the point of departure and return for skiers is directly below.

The scene is even more memorable at night, sitting in the subdued light of the dining room, with its solarium windows. The floodlit slopes with skiers flitting in and out of the shadows creates an engaging picture. It is even more magical on a snowy evening, when the lights of the village, which wraps around the hill rising across the lake, flicker through.

Traditional Canadian buffet-style breakfasts feature "hot" and "cold" tables. There are fewer courses at lunch than at dinner but almost as many choices. Entrées covering every taste or dietary need are included in the five-course evening meal. Le Chantecler has chosen to stay with continental cuisine; it is a gastronomic treat without parallel and exquisitely executed.

Rooms are modern, with whirlpool baths, phones and TV, but enriched by handcrafted, traditional furniture. In addition to the large living room with fireplace at the entrance, there is another sizable room off the main corridor for reading or table games. The cocktail lounge sits between the terrace and the dining room and has musical entertainment in the evening. Several shops, including massage and beauty salon, cater to many needs.

In 1991 the chamber of commerce honored the hotel for its contribution, signaling the community's support for

141

*The entrance is built into
an ancient wooden tower.*

Le Chantecler's expansion. There can
be no doubt that this resort keeps
Sainte-Adèle standing at "the Crest,"
too.

SKIING AT
LE CHANTECLER

*Downhill and telemark skiers simply
walk out and slide down to one of two
base lifts at the foot of the hill near the
lake. Cross country types can warm up
by climbing a short distance past the*

condominiums along one of the downhill
trails and then cross under the lift line
to enter the forest.

The cross country trails, laid out in the
1970s through Chantecler property lying
directly behind the hotel, now traverse
parts of a new 18-hole golf course being
developed adjacent to the ski lifts.
Skinny board skiers have the fun of crossing and re-crossing the lifts and in one
place climb almost as high as one of the
summits. The total of ten kilometers
combining in-woods and open terrain is
rated novice and intermediate, but that
belies the variation in grade that makes
them interesting and challenging.

The trails hook into a very extensive
network surrounding Sainte-Adèle. Avid
skier Elizabeth Fraichen, who for years
had explored the old unused hiking paths
and logging roads now incorporated in
the system, was one of the prime movers
in organizing the community effort to
maintain them. The hotel calls on her to
serve as a guide for skiers through the
lake and cottage district.

All skiers are served by the same ski
shop, on the level directly below the
main entrance of the hotel. The cafteria
has a complete lunch menu where non-
skiers may eat as well. A large ski lodge
at the base of the fourth and largest
mountain provides complete services and
is the preferred entrance for day-skiers.

There are so many recreation facilities
that it is hard not to be diverted—a
swimming pool, exercise rooms, racquet
and handball courts, organized contests,
theme parties, and musical entertainment.

*Left, the horse-drawn
sleigh rides are fun.*

Be sure and bring your
French-English pocket dictionary
for use on the trails, which
are well marked.

Right, the guest rooms are
furnished with traditional
French Canadian pine.

LE CHÂTEAU MONTEBELLO

A triumph of rustic architecture and sophisticated winter sports

The monumental seventy-foot centerpeice of the three-story rotunda.

ENTERING the Château Montebello is like walking onto a movie set. A 70-foot chimney soars to the ceiling of a three-floor rotunda, the centerpiece of four wings arranged in star fashion around it—the largest log building in the world. An exclusive private club from 1930 until 1970, it is only one of the premier properties operated by Canadian Pacific Hotels.

The sheer size of this magnificent structure and the elegance of its interior design is overwhelming. Remarkably, the feeling of being connected with the earth normally associated with a cozy log cabin is imparted here as well. The logs and other fine woods used in paneling and furnishings, glowing with age and the years of careful attention, enrich the effect.

The secret of success for any hostelry lies with the staff. The number of years many have served is astounding. The loyalty of Montebello employees is bound up with pride in community—proof of the connection between the hotel and its locality.

Right, chef Luc Montagne, who presides over the three-story main dining room, below.

Far from being a cloistered place, each year the Château becomes the logistical headquarters for the overnight leg of the famous Canadian Ski Marathon, which attracts a thousand skiers.

Equally prized for their tradition are the annual curling championships, among them the senior ladies' Sewell Bonspiel, which has passed its 60th anniversary. Clubs wait years for an opening.

One need not leave the Château for anything from a fur jacket to a newspaper. The indoor sports center (pool, exercise rooms, and courts) is reached by an underground tunnel from the lobby.

Sumptuous does not begin to describe the food. A day could be devoted to the **145** breakfast buffet. Similarly, lunch brings seemingly endless choices; dinner is a feast. This is truly international cuisine, and underscores the fact that CP hotels reach for international recognition.

The main dining room also has a three-story ceiling, although it is set on a level below the lobby. Around the first balcony are huge murals depicting Canadian history and on the next level, the shields of the ten Canadian provinces. It is easy to imagine government dignitaries descending the broad staircase, set off by totem sculptures, during the NATO summit hosted here in 1983.

A reading of history reveals that this is a most romantic setting. At breakfast in an alcove looking out over the frozen river, one can reminisce that the Ottawa River was the storied gateway to the interior when European explorers began looking for the route to Cathay. In 1613, French explorer Nicolas Vignan traversed it on his way to the Great Lakes and the Mississippi. He was followed by the famed coureurs de bois, who opened up the continent.

SKIING AT CHATEAU MONTEBELLO

The Chateau ski shop shares space with the curling rinks. The snack bar/lounge

The ancient Scottish-Canadian game of curling is practiced assiduously.

Guest rooms are comfortable, with all the amenities.

serves both. Equipment for rental or purchase and information about other activities like skating, tobogganing, and sleigh rides are centered here.

Two novice trails are laid out on the grounds around the hotel, where there are also walking paths and a skating rink. The major trail system is laid out around the golf course, about a mile by car; ambitious skiers can take a more direct trail from the hotel.

The Seigneury Club property extends for miles back into the bush on the north side of the river; the hills crowd close to the shore here. Predominantly intermediate skiing is found near the course and on roads unused in winter surrounding it. Four intermediate and two advanced trails are tracked and groomed, wide enough for skating.

Leaving the broad shelf of land at the golf club, one trail swings over a low mountain, past a few of the chalets and vacation homes built there. Once on top, the terrain opens up again and then drops back down into a shallow valley, creating a pleasantly varied landscape.

Unusual diversions like snowmobile trips to a deer sanctuary and all-day excursions by dogsled, both including lunch, can be arranged for a fee. Or, one can go ice fishing, learn trapping from a guide, and in season, visit a maple sugar shack.

Montebello offers many activities, such as ice skating and cross country skiing but the monumental inn buildings are always omnipresent.

One good way to get away from it all is to take a horse-drawn sleigh ride as shown at left.

Far Hills Inn is one of
Canada's premier resorts,
and it is especially
beautiful in the winter time.

*Right, the dining room, whose
cuisine sets levels of excellence
difficult to duplicate elsewhere.*

*Left, innkeepers
David and Louise Pemberton Smith,
who are indispensable.*

FAR HILLS INN

Savor the best that Canada has to offer

GRACIOUS SURROUNDINGS might be the best way to describe Far Hills Inn: elegant but not overwhelming . . . an atmosphere that puts one at ease immediately . . . fabulous food . . . and the most extensive cross country trail system in the Laurentians. The distinctive Canadian architecture—stonework facing on the lower half of the buildings, clapboards above and steep roofs with gabled windows—is superbly suited to the wooded, mountainside setting. Cedar Lodge and Spruce Lodge, both containing meeting rooms and lodgings, have been added since the main inn was built in 1940.

With Mount Iceberg rising at its back, the inn has a 180-degree vista of nearby Lake Raymond and the low peaks surrounding it.

The living room has a comfortable, lived-in look. There are seating arrangements of handmade, wood-frame couches and chairs with overstuffed cushions; a bank of windows looks out on the terraced swimming pool. Murals on the fireplace wall, painted by Kurt Maurer, a Swiss neighbor, depict typical rural scenes. Other murals can be found in unexpected places such as a hallway or a bedroom.

The cocktail lounge has a number of small tables grouped around a semicircular bar and another mural-decorated fireplace. At the far end, picture windows extend the view toward the Far Hills.

David and Louise Pemberton Smith have improved the inn steadily since acquiring it in 1975. For the past few years, David has concentrated on bringing the Provincial government's rating of the dining room to the highest level—four forks—and he reached that goal last year. The cuisine is nouvelle but not extreme, changing to meet the health-conscious standards of today.

Louise sets the tone for the treatment of guests. She is everywhere, overseeing details and directing the staff with the courtesy and concern that she and David hope will be transmitted to guests. The employees' respect for her is evident, and the philosophy works splendidly.

The easy informality gives little indication of the professionalism behind the scenes. Far Hills has been chosen to host NATO meetings and international gatherings, as well as top-level business conferences and seminars. It is only about an hour from Montreal and a short drive from the northern expressway, but the nature of these wooded hills engenders a total change in outlook.

There are many alternatives . . . the indoor swimming pool, sauna, and recreation room with billiards, ping pong, and card tables. David, a six-time na-

There are a variety of trails to take, but this is where everyone starts.

tional squash doubles champion, is particularly proud of the courts at the clubhouse, a short walk down the road. Luncheon is served there, as well as in the cocktail lounge.

A most charming recent addition is the small exhibit of watercolor paintings done by David's aunt, the late Freda Pemberton Smith, who gained national recognition late in her life.

SKIING AT FAR HILLS INN

In the twenties and thirties, the legendary Herman "Jackrabbit" Smith-Johann-

sen began to lay out the Maple Leaf Trail, which he envisioned would extend from Montreal through the Laurentians, so that everyone could get out into the bush and enjoy his sport. If this grandfather of Canadian skiing could head north on it today, he probably would not get beyond Far Hills, where his spiritual successors have carried on his dream.

The inn occupies 300 acres, and another 3000 acres of woodlands and lakes around the villages of Val Morin and Val David are spun with a web of white tracks. There are more than 100 kilometers of trails, about half of them groomed. Five kilometers are prepared for skating and another 15 are double-tracked and wide. Guides are suggested when taking the longer ones into the backcountry.

David has a minimum of four teaching professionals at the ski center at all times, qualified to teach classic, skating, or telemark technique. Next to the center is a small practice slope. The ski shop has equipment for all kinds of skiing and full repair services.

Beginning skiers have more extensive entrée to the woods than in most areas. Improving to the intermediate level is a great incentive, because these trails have wonderful views, beginning with a manageable route to the top of Iceberg. It rises abruptly and is rimmed by two lakes. The Pemberton circles a nearby peak of that name; it was used as a training and racing trail, and is doubly satisfying for the recreational skier. It's best to study the landscape on the way up, because it whips by quickly on the downhills!

A striking view of cross country skiers enjoying themselves.

Left, the pool is the centerpiece of the Recreation Center.

Olympian Pierre Harvey leads the way past one of the snug log cabins that make up the Auberge.

Left, the tracking and grooming is never-ending.

L'AUBERGE DU FONDEUR

Set in a provincial park with superb skiing

BEING in the woods on skis during the day only intensifies one's desire for more. For those who would like the experience of staying in a remote setting without the trouble of getting there, Parc du Mont-Sainte-Anne has an answer: its wilderness lodge, L'Auberge du Fondeur, is literally right on the cross country network.

For planners in the crown corporation set up by the provincial government to operate its parks, opening the lodge was something of an experiment. They've been amazed by the response, particularly from abroad. But Canada is fast discovering that "eco-tourism," vacations involving natural and scenic wonders, is one of its major attractions. Millions of dollars have gone into making the Mont-Sainte-Anne skiing facilities among the best on the continent.

The mountain, half an hour from Quebec City, is the first major peak in the Laurentian Shield, among the oldest mountains in the world. The entrance to the park lies at the edge of the village of Saint Ferreol-les-Neiges, beyond the alpine center. The access road climbs steadily, past the complete cross country center, and winds around a shoulder of the mountain, about midway up a broad valley.

The low, modern building blends into the landscape. Originally used for conducting international competitions, it has two levels of picture windows looking out on the track, which is set extra wide in a long meadow to accommodate starting lanes. Indoors and outdoors seem to meld through the glass.

Host Bernard Noel has the uncommon gift of making everyone feel at home, overcoming language or social barriers by his affability. This is primar-

Warm wood walls and huge wooden beams in the lounge are a modern contrast to the log cabins.

153

Impeccable grooming and fantastic scenery add to the popularity of the Auberge.

ily a do-it-yourself operation; linens and towels are distributed and guests make up their own beds. Some rooms are dormitories and a few have bunks and beds, suited to a family or group. Baths and the sauna are shared.

The main common room extends almost the full length of the building, divided by a bar where beverages including alcohol are dispensed. A fireplace with accompanying couches and easy chairs fills one end; a few small tables with chairs are arranged elsewhere, with space left near the entrance for parking gear. Weather, temperature, and trail conditions are posted on the information board here every morning.

A full breakfast is served, but after that guests are on their own. Most choose to buy or bring food and share preparations in the kitchen (storage space is provided). This increases the camaraderie and leads to shared excursions. Some guests occasionally return to civilization to dine out.

Coming back to the inn and the glow of floodlit tracks, rimmed by trees, it is easy to regain the sense of seclusion. Starlit nights can be spectacular.

All in all, this is roughing it the easy way.

SKIING AT L'AUBERGE DU FONDEUR

The statistics are impressive for this largest cross country center in Canada, which has been blessed by nature with a bountiful supply of beautiful snow every winter for the last twenty years. There are 70 square kilometers of land in the park, and 214 kilometers of double-tracked trails, almost half of them prepared for skating.

About two kilometers below the auberge on a novice trail is the Chalet du rang Saint-Julien, a two-story center for services. It has a cafeteria, ski shop, waxing room, showers, first aid clinic, and ski school. Eight heated shelters are sprinkled about the trail system.

Part of the network leading from the center lies on gently rolling terrain along the Jean-Larose River and the base of Mont-Ferreol. They are labeled easy and offer many choices for distance; one short swing of three kilometers is close to the center.

Across the access road, a more difficult trail climbs to a ridge above the auberge and then dips down again to meet the stream farther down. A short circuit with uphill climbing brings the skier back to the center. A pleasant longer route, also rated more difficult, winds gradually downhill through the woods along the stream to the alpine center. On weekends and holidays, a free bus runs from there to the cross country center in the morning and returns skiers in the afternoon.

Near the auberge, the trails that qualify the center for international competition trace the long valleys lying behind Mont-Sainte-Anne and circle the high bluffs lying east of it, with magnificent views of the St. Lawrence River valley. Other trails labeled most difficult are found deep in the bush to the north, but the access trails are manageable by novice and intermediate skiers with stamina. Two wilderness overnight trips requiring guides can also be arranged.

*Overlooking Murray Bay,
and the St. Lawrence, the
inn was formerly the summer
home of the Ohio Taft family,
and has been beautifully restored
by the present innkeeper.
The guest rooms shown here
give some idea of the quality
of workmanship and furnishings
that have gone into the inn.*

AUBERGE DES 3 CANARDS

Exciting views of the St. Lawrence River

THE SWEEPING grandeur of the landscape east of Quebec City, will long linger in the mind. The highway swoops and turns over the enfolded hills, occasionally giving a glimpse of the mighty St. Lawrence River.

At the mouth of the Malbie River, the shore road turns south to Pointe au Pic, along what was formerly known as Murray Bay. "Like Nirvana . . . not so much a place as a state of mind," wrote Tim Porteous, Canadian travel writer, of summers there. Its elegant unpretentiousness is evident even in winter.

According to one theory, "The Three Ducks" may be a French version of "The Three Docs," for the three physicians who originally opened the inn during the 1950s. At least the present name, accented by stylized sculptures within the inn, makes a connection with the river. The bay spreads out several hundred feet below the broad expanse of lawns, which protect the view.

At night, the lights around the north shore to Cap-a-L'Aigle are a sparkling panorama; in daylight, the shifting colors and mists are mesmerizing. Although there is snow from mid-November to April, the bay never freezes. The south shore is about thirteen miles away.

In the late 19th century, when Murray Bay was called the Newport of Canada, the inn was first the summer home of the Taft family of Ohio and later of the Galts of Montreal. Giant beams and pine paneling from British Columbia were used throughout the three-story building. The woodwork has been brought back to its former beauty by innkeeper Pierre Marchand, its scent noticeable immediately upon entering.

LOUISE PAQUIN PHOTOS

The living room, with several conversation areas laid out with bentwood furniture, fills almost the entire front corner of the 70-foot by 90-foot building. A small bar separates it from the dining room, which is divided into two sections, both with high windows. Throughout the inn, paintings by local artists imbue a sense of life here over the years.

Most of the bedrooms in the inn have fireplaces and sitting areas with televisions. Imaginative use has been made of space, for example, in a two-level, bed-sitting arrangement. Additional rooms are found in the motel adjacent to the inn, overlooking the tennis courts and pool.

Last year the inn received the bronze award for its five-course French cuisine under the strict rating system of the provincial government. The inn's high standards, using fresh products from the region, contributes to its success in hosting group meetings. There are both table d'hôte and à la carte menus.

Monsieur Marchand was an engineer with a construction firm in Quebec City when he decided about ten years ago to pursue his dream of owning an inn. Instead of being a part-time job, he soon found this to be an all-consuming occupation.

SKIING AT AUBERGE DES TROIS CANARDS

Skiing at Les Trois Canards runs the gamut from sliding around on the front lawn, which has a dandy slope, to exploring Charlevoix Region backcountry with a guide on skis, snowshoes, dogsled or snowmobile.

There is more social activity at the community ski center on Mont Grand-Fonds, which stands a surprising 2200 feet in elevation only a short distance inland. The alpine trails have a thousand-foot descent.

Ticket booth and ski shop are located in a small building beside the main lodge, which has cafeteria and eating space downstairs and a cocktail lounge above. A separate warming hut for cross country skiers sits next to the trail entrance.

A beginner trail moves one away from the bustle immediately into undulating terrain. Interesting changes in ground cover and landscape, easy climbs, and downhill stretches of varying length mark this pleasant, 7-kilometer loop. A ski hut about halfway around is the lunch and warming stop.

The intermediate trails climb beyond this to a plateau where a total of 50 kilometers can be skied by degrees. A good-sized lake lies in the middle of three loops. Two warming cabins (all have stoves and a water supply) are located along them.

Expert trails extend into more rugged country, with another hut and small lakes for goals. More expert trails (they total 83 kilometers) climb the back side of the mountain, leaving the access trail early on.

For an afternoon off, the river route to Baie-St.-Paul winds through picturesque villages where regional artists and crafts people can be found.

Both flat and undulating terrain appeal to all levels of cross country skier.

Left, the best looking lobster you ever saw! The inn's high standards earned its cuisine a bronze medal in 1990.

VILLA BELLEVUE RESORT & SPA

Three generations of Dubois are aiming at perfection

These skiers look very professional, and they could be, as the Mont Tremblant area has drawn the very best of skiers ever since the 1930s.

A LEGEND recounts that this mountain was the home of the mighty Manitou, God of the Wilderness, whose wrath could make the very ground tremble—hence Mont Tremblant. Any quaking today only relates to tired knees in powdered snow and rumbling machinery carrying skiers up to challenge Manitou himself.

If Sun Valley, Idaho, was the first haven for skiing "jet-setters" (who traveled by train then), this resort, opened in 1938, could claim to be the second. Herman "Jackrabbit" Smith-Johannsen, honored figure of Canadian skiing, and members of the Red Bird Ski Club of Montreal were breaking out trails here in the 1920s. The first official Quebec Kandahar, oldest alpine race in North America, was held in 1932 on Tremblant. A visit by Philadelphian Joe Ryan and his pal, Lowell Thomas, led to Ryan's decision to build "the biggest ski center in the East."

The renascence of cross country skiing in the Seventies helped bring winter back as the premier season in this part of the Laurentians.

Among the hotels and inns built early in the century on the lakes sprinkled about the mountain was a small one on Lac Ouimet. It was acquired in 1925 by Euclide Dubois, son of a pioneer settler, who continued his father's work as logger and sawmill operator, and built the church in Mont Tremblant founded by the famous "skiing priest," Fr. Charles-Hector Deslauniers.

The third generation of this family is now operating the inn: Serge, who joined his father in 1964; Luc, in 1976, Robert, in 1981; and later Suzanne, who took over the business office. Papa René oversees them and the entire operation in his own unobtrusive way.

To say that they have moved with the times is an understatement. A modern indoor sports complex with swimming pool, exercise and massage rooms, sauna and steam baths has been installed; above are up-to-date bedrooms with fireplaces. At the heart of the

The ski shop attracts everyone.

traditional inn building is a large living room; a split-level dining room incorporates the white stucco walls of the old exterior. On the opposite side of the main common room is a cocktail lounge with dance floor, where a good deal of organized entertainment is concocted.

From this center, the accommodations fan out to a connected motel that arcs around the lakefront. Cottage condominiums, designed to be unobtrusive, are located across the main highway, and share the inn's facilities.

The food at the Villa is a magnet, even if skiers go flying off during the day. The buffet breakfast is substantial enough to carry one through, but lunch is also served. The continental cuisine with French influences is suited to North American tastes and one can indulge in a hearty way.

SKIING AT
VILLA BELLEVUE

When Luc returned in 1976 from a three-year stint as head coach of the national alpine team, having taken Canada to an Olympic gold medal, cross country skiing was just taking off. He was instrumental in getting the permission of landowners to make possible the 90-kilometer system that now extends from Saint-Jovite, five miles south, to Mont Tremblant, four miles northwest.

From the inn, one can ski into one of the villages for lunch or stop at an inn along the way. There is free bus service connecting all the resorts with the Mont Tremblant Ski Center. Lift tickets can be picked up at the inn, which has its own ski shop for technical assistance and gear.

Both alpine and cross country skiing can be more structured at Villa Bellevue, if desired. Midweek packages involve

The white stucco walls of the original inn, on the left, blend with the deep snowbanks surrounding the inn. On the right is the more modern indoor sports complex, with guest rooms above that have all the latest amenities.

daily lessons; the nordic types, divided according to ability, are taken to different parts of the system each day. A special lunch tour to Mont Tremblant Park is held at the end of the week. The bonus is the social activities that are built into the program, involving videos, films, contests and celebratory parties.

Luc, who was alpine race chairman for the Calgary Olympics, supervises an impressive array of instructors. He believes that cross country skiing was presented as too easy and accessible in its early days. "People would find the sport more exciting if they could do it better," he says. His pros are prepared to match their teaching to any level.

There are rivers to follow, woods to explore, and mountains to climb—more than enough to keep anyone interested. **163**

PENNSYLVANIA

THE STERLING INN. Rte. 191, South Sterling, PA 18460; (800) 523-8200; Fax (717) 676-9786; Ron and Mary Kay Logan, innkeepers. Open all year. **Rates:** $75 to $85 per person single occupancy, MAP; $65 to $95 per person double occupancy, MAP; lunch available. **Accommodations:** 40 rooms, 12 suites, 2 cabins, all with private baths. Hearthstone Dining Room and Terrace Pub at guests' disposal. Children welcome; no pets; non-smoking dining room; French spoken; Visa, MasterCard, American Express. **Winter facilities:** cross country skiing, sledding, ice skating, horse-drawn sleigh rides, tobogganing, indoor swimming pool and Jacuzzi. **Ski shop:** equipment rental and sales, guide service, ski instruction, refreshments, warming huts, medical and first aid services.

Directions: from I-84 take exit 6 to Rte. 507 south for 3 miles to Rte. 191 south for 3 miles to inn. From I-80 west take exit 50 to Rte. 191 north for 25 miles to inn. From I-80 east take Rte. 380 to Rte. 423 north to Rte. 191 north for 1/2 mile to inn.

THE INN AT STARLIGHT LAKE, P.O. Box 27, Starlight, PA 18461; (800) 248-2519; (717) 798-2519; Jack and Judy McMahon, inkeepers. Open all year except for 2 weeks from the last Sunday in March. **Rates:** $64 to $94 single MAP; $110 to $154 double MAP. **Accommodations:** 26 rooms in main house, cottages and family house, most with private baths. One suite has a double whirlpool bath. Restaurant serves full breakfast and lunch and dinner to guests and public. Liquor served. BYOB in rooms only. Children welcome; no pets; smoking allowed except in restricted part of dining room; Visa, MasterCard. **Winter facilities:** cross country skiing, ice skating at inn; downhill areas nearby. **Ski shop:** equipment rental and sales, ski instruction, guide service by appointment, medical and first aid services, refreshments.

Directions: from New York and New Jersey take Rte. 17 west to Hancock, NY to exit 87 onto PA Rte. 191 south for a few miles to Rte. 370 to Starlight. From Philadelphia and southern Pennsylvania take any convenient route north to Scranton. From Scranton take Rte. 6 west to Rte. 171 north to Rte. 370 east to Starlight.

NEW YORK

FRIENDS LAKE INN, Friends Lake Rd. Chestertown, NY 12817; (518) 494-4751; Fax (518) 494-7423; Sharon and Greg Taylor. Open all year. **Rates:** $130 per couple MAP. **Accommodations:** 11 rooms, 6 suites, 2 cabins, all with private baths. Full restaurant service, lakeview bar, and award-winning wine list. Children welcome; no pets; smoking allowed; Visa, MasterCard. **Winter facilities:** 25 miles of beginner, intermediate, and expert terrain for cross country skiing. **Ski shop:** equipment rental and sales, guide service, ski instruction, refreshments, warming huts, medical and first aid services.

Directions: from south take I-87 north to exit 23 onto Rte. 9 through Warrensburg to Rte. 28 north. Approx. 5 miles to Friends Lake Road, turn right to inn. From north take I-87 south to exit 25 onto Rte. 8 west for 2 1/2 miles to Friends Lake Road. Turn left but bear right at each fork in the road to the inn.

CROSS COUNTRY SKI INNS

HIGHWINDS INN, P.O. Box 370, Barton Mines Rd., North River, NY 12856; (518) 251-3760; Kimberly A. Repscha, innkeeper. Open all year except the month of November. **Rates:** $100 double B & B, $150 double MAP. **Accommodations:** 4 rooms sharing 2 baths, and 2 remote wilderness cabins. Restaurant also open to the public. BYOB for liquor. Children over 6 welcome; no pets; smoking in living room only; Visa, MasterCard; Spanish spoken. **Winter facilities:** complete cross country touring center. **Ski shop:** equipment rental and sales, guide service, ski instruction, refreshments, warming huts, medical and first aid services.

Directions: from I-87 going north or south, take exit 23 onto Rte. 9 north through Warrensburg to Rte. 28. Follow signs to Gore Mountain ski area and North River 5 miles beyond North Creek. Turn left on Barton Mines Rd. at North River General Store and drive 5 miles up the mountain to inn. Bus pickup at Warrensburg.

GARNET HILL LODGE, 13th Lake Road, North River, NY 12856; (518) 251-2821; George and Mary Heim, innkeepers. Open all year. **Rates:** $65 to $90 per person MAP. **Accommodations:** 27 rooms with private baths. Vacation home rentals available. Restaurant serves 3 meals daily to guests and public; liquor served. Children welcome; no pets; smoking in designated areas; Visa, MasterCard, personal checks. **Winter facilities:** full service cross country ski center with 54 km. of groomed trails, unlimited wilderness skiing, guided tours, shuttle bus service, kids program, night skiing. **Ski shop:** equipment rental and sales, guide service, daily ski instruction, refreshments, medical and first aid services, warming huts.

Directions: from Albany take I-87 north to exit 23 at Warrensburg and go north on Rte. 9 to Rte. 28. Go north on Rte. 28 for 22 miles to North River and turn left onto 13th Lake Road for 5 miles to lodge. Bus pickups at Warrensburg.

BARK EATER INN, P.O. Box 139, Alstead Hill Rd., Keene, NY 12942; (518) 576-2221; Fax (518) 576-2071; Joe-Pete Wilson, owner; Jodi Downs, business mgr. Open all year. **Rates:** (including breakfast) $67.50 to $87.50 single; $45 to $55 per person double. **Accommodations:** 17 rooms, 6 with private baths and 11 sharing 4 baths. 5-course gourmet dinner available by reservation, served family style. No bar, BYOB. Children welcome; no pets; smoking restricted; some French spoken; Visa, MasterCard, American Express. **Winter facilities:** 20 km. of cross country ski trails, with 2 warming rooms and wax room. Horseback riding year round, and hay and sleigh rides available. **Ski shop:** equipment rental and sales, guide service, ski instruction, refreshments, medical and first aid services, warming huts.

Directions: from Albany on I-87 north, take exit 30 and go left on Rte. 73 west towards Lake Placid for approx. 26 miles. Watch for Bark Eater sign on right and turn at Alstead Hill Rd. Inn is 1/4 mile on left.

RATES: The rates shown here are current rates and are subject to change. The rates shown for **Canadian inns** are in Canadian dollars.

MASSACHUSETTS

THE WEATHERVANE INN, P.O. Box 388, South Egremont, MA 01258; (413) 528-9580; Fax (413) 528-1713; Anne and Vincent Murphy, innkeepers. Open all year. **Rates:** $95 B & B per room; $160 MAP per room. **Accommodations:** 11 rooms with private baths and choice of king, queen, or twin beds. Dining room open to guests and public on weekends; midweek for guests only upon request; bar open to guests at all times. Children over 7 welcome; no pets; smoking restricted; Visa, MasterCard, American Express. **Winter facilities:** Butternut Basin has groomed trails and 2 state forests provide maps for their cross country trails. **Ski shop:** recommend Kenver Ltd. in South Egremont for rental and sales.

Directions: located in southern Berkshires 3 miles west of Barrington, Mass., on Rte. 23. Approx. 2½ hours from Boston or NYC.

VERMONT

THE HERMITAGE INN, Coldbrook Road, Wilmington, VT 05363; (802) 464-3511; Fax (802) 464-2688; James L. McGovern, Innkeeper. Open all year. **Rates:** $65 to $100 per person double occupancy, MAP. **Accommodations:** 29 rooms, 25 with private baths, 4 sharing. Restaurant serves dinner nightly, soup and sandwich daily in winter, brunch on holidays and weekends to guests and public. Liquor served. Children welcome (same rates apply); no pets; French and German spoken; all major credit cards. **Winter facilities:** full touring center with 50 km of groomed trails; Sporting Clays course; Ridge Trail tours. **Ski shop:** equipment rental; ski instruction; guide service; snowshoe rental; telemark rental and lessons; first aid.

Directions: from Wilmington go 2½ miles on Rte. 100 north and turn left onto Coldbrook Road. Go 3 miles and Hermitage is on the left. Private plane pickup from Mt. Snow Airport available.

WINDHAM HILL INN, RR 1, Box 44, West Townshend, VT 05359; (802) 874-4080; Fax (802) 874-4976; Ken and Linda Busteed, innkeepers. Open May through Oct., Thanksgiving, and Dec. through March. **Rates:** $110 to $120 single MAP; $160 to $170 double MAP. **Accommodations:** 15 rooms with private baths. Meals served to guests only, including full liquor license. Children over 12 welcome; no pets; no smoking; Visa, MasterCard. **Winter facilities:** cross country skiing and ice skating. **Ski shop:** equipment rental and sales, guide service, ski instruction at learning center, refreshments.

Directions: from I-91 north take Vermont exit 2 to Rte. 30 north. Inn is north of Brattleboro off Rte. 30. Entering village of West Townshend, look for Windham Hill Inn directional sign. 3/10 miles beyond sign, turn right opposite the country store. Go up hill for 1¼ miles to access road to inn on your right. Southbound on Rte. 30 the country store where you turn is ½ mile beyond the directional sign.

THREE MOUNTAIN INN, Box 180 S, Jamaica, VT 05343; (802) 874-4140; Charles and Elaine Murray, owners. Open mid-Dec. through March and Mid-May through October. **Rates:** $75 to $95 per person MAP with special reduced-rate midweek packages. **Accommodations:** 16 rooms, 1 suite, 1 cabin, all with private baths. Full bar; dining room with a variety of appetizer, entrée and dessert choices, and an excellent wine list. Well-behaved children welcome; no pets; smoking in common areas, but not in guest rooms and dining room; American Express and personal checks. **Winter facilities:** 8 cross country touring centers within 20 minutes and Jamaica State Park just a short walk. Ice skating, alpine skiing, and sledding nearby. **Ski shop:** equipment rental and sales, guide service, ski instruction, medical and first aid services, and warming huts all available at the touring centers nearby.

Directions: from I-91 north take 2nd Brattleboro exit to Rte. 30 north and go 28 miles to Jamaica. From Albany take Rte. 9 to Bennington and Rte. 7 to Manchester and Rte. 30 to Jamaica.

ROWELL'S INN, RR 1, Box 267D, Chester, VT 05143; (802) 875-3658; Beth and Lee Davis, owners. Open all year except April and first 2 weeks of Nov. **Rates:** $140 double MAP. **Accommodations:** 6 rooms with private baths. Dining room and Tavern Room for guests only. Children over twelve welcome; no pets; smoking with consideration for others is permitted; assorted Vermont dialects spoken; no credit cards. **Winter facilities:** inn-to-inn cross country tours arranged; many cross country touring centers close by, with complete ski shop services.

Directions: located on Rte. 11 in Simonsville 7 miles west of Chester and 7 miles east of Londonderry. From I-91 take exit 6 to Rte. 103 for 8 miles into Chester. Take Rte. 11 7 miles west to Simonsville.

WOODSTOCK INN AND RESORT: 14 The Green, Woodstock, VT 05091; for reservations (800) 448-7900; other calls to (802) 457-1100; Fax (802) 457-3824; Chet Williamson, general manager. Open all year. **Rates:** $125 to $245 double to 5/24/92, no meals included. **Accommodations:** 139 rooms, 7 suites, all with private baths. Tavern, 2 dining rooms, and function rooms at inn; bar, lounge, and restaurant at each of 3 sports locations. Children welcome; no pets; smoking allowed, non-smoking rooms available; Visa, MasterCard, American Express. **Winter facilities:** Woodstock Ski Touring Center and Suicide Six Ski Area all under resort management. Indoor Sports Center at resort features swimming, sauna, whirlpool, massage, tennis, squash, racquet ball, Nautilus fitness center, and outdoor platform tennis. **Ski shop:** equipment rental and sales, guide service, ski instruction, medical and first aid services, warming huts, and refreshments that include bar, full luncheon, and catering for private functions.

Directions: from junction of I-89 and I-91 in White River Junction, Vt., go west on I-89 to exit 1 onto Rte. 4 for 13 miles to Woodstock. At Village Green, inn is on left corner of Rte. 106. Ski Touring Center is ½ mile south on Rte. 106.

MOUNTAIN TOP INN AND CROSS COUNTRY SKI RESORT, Mountain Top Road, Chittenden, VT 05737; (800) 445-2100; (802) 483-2311; Fax (802) 483-6373; William Wolfe, manager. Open all year. **Rates:** $65 to $135 per person double occupancy, not including meals. **Accommodations:** 33 rooms and 22 chalets and cottages, all with private baths. Outstanding views from dining room, with fireplace, and cocktail lounge, with fireplace. Children welcome; no pets; smoking allowed but not in dining room; Spanish, French, German spoken; Visa, MasterCard, Amnerican Express. **Winter facilities:** 110 km of cross country trails, 70 km of which are groomed daily. Horsedrawn sleighrides, ice skating day or night, sledding, sauna, whirlpool. Snowmaking equipment on hand. **Ski shop:** equipment rental and sales, ski instruction, refreshments, medical and first aid services, 3 warming huts.

Directions: from Rutland, Vt., take Rte. 7 north to Chittenden Rd. and go north through Chittenden to inn overlooking the reservoir.

THE OLD CUTTER INN, RR 1, Box 62, East Burke, VT 05832; (802) 626-5152; Fritz and Marti Walther, owners. Closed during off-season months of April and November. **Rates:** (room only) $40 to $50 single; $48 to $60 double; (MAP) $95 per person for 2 days; 3, 4, and 5 day packages also available. **Accommodations:** 9 rooms, 5 with private baths and 4 sharing; 1 suite with 2 bedrooms, living room, kitchen, fireplace, and bath. Full dinner menu featuring Swiss cuisine, wine list, and homemade desserts. Breakfast and Sunday brunch, but no lunch served. Bar, with pub menu. Restaurant closed on Wednesdays. Children welcome; pets welcome; smoking allowed; French, Swiss, German, and a little Italian spoken; Visa, MasterCard. **Winter facilities:** alpine and nordic skiing at nearby Burke Mountain Ski Resort. Sledding, snowshoeing, sleigh rides, ice skating, ice fishing. **Ski shop** at Burke Mountain has equipment sales and rental, ski instruction, refreshments, medical and first aid services, and warming huts.

Directions: from St. Johnsbury take US-5 north to Rte. 114 northeast to East Burke. Go through town and take Burke Mountain Access Road for 2 miles to inn.

EDSON HILL MANOR, 1500 Edson Hill Road, Stowe, VT 05672; (800) 621-0284; (802) 253-7371; Eric and Jane Lande, owners; Bob Howd, general manager. Open all year. **Rates:** $79 to $89 per person per night, MAP; $89 to $99 on Presidents' Day and the week between Christmas and New Year's. **Accommodations:** 24 rooms; 9 in manor and 15 in carriage houses, 20 with fireplaces, 22 with private baths and 2 sharing. Restaurant serves 3 meals to guests and public; liquor served. Children welcome; no pets; smoking allowed; Visa, MasterCard, American Express. **Winter facilities:** cross country skiing on inn's own 40 km of trails for novice, intermediate, and advanced difficulties. Sleighrides, tobogganing, and ice skating on ponds. **Ski shop:** nearby equipment rental and sales, ski instruction, guide service, waxing and repairs.

Directions: from I-89 south take exit 10 to Rte. 100 north for 10 miles to Rte. 108 north for 3.1 miles to Edson Hill Road. Turn right for 2 miles to inn. Shuttlebus from Burlington to Stowe for bus, Amtrak, and plane travelers.

HIGHLAND LODGE, Caspian Lake, Greensboro, VT 05841; (802) 533-2647; The Smith Family (David, Wilhelmina, Alex), innkeepers. Winter season Dec. 21 to March 10. **Rates:** $80 to $110 single MAP; $140 to $175 double per couple MAP. (Rates include 15% service charge.) **Accommodations:** 10 rooms and 4 winterized cabins, all with private baths. Excellent dining in 2 cozy dining rooms, with beer and wine served. Children welcome; no pets; no smoking in common areas; Dutch and French spoken; Visa, MasterCard. **Winter facilities:** sledding, tobogganing, and cross counry skiing on 40 miles of roller packed, track-set trails included in rates. **Ski shop:** equipment rental and sales, guide service, ski instruction, refreshments.

Directions: from south on I-91 exit at. St. Johnsbury onto Rte. 15/US-2 west for 10 miles to West Danville. Take Rte. 15 northwest 11 miles to Rte. 16 north for 2 miles to East Hardwick. Turn west and follow signs for 4 miles to Greensboro. From Quebec on I-91 south exit at Barton onto Rte. 16 south for 16 miles to Greensboro Bend. Turn west and follow signs for 3 miles to Greensboro. *From Greensboro take East Craftsbury road north; leaving Greensboro bear left and keep left for 2 miles to lodge.*

THE INN ON THE COMMON, Box 75, Main Street, Craftsbury Common, VT 05827; (800) 521-2233; (802) 586-9619; Fax (802) 586-2249; Penny and Michael Schmitt, innkeepers. Open all year. **Rates:** $190 to $250 double MAP. **Accommodations:** 15 rooms and 1 suite, all with private baths. Complete meal and liquor service, with excellent wine cellar. Children welcome, pets welcome; smoking allowed except in dining room; Visa, MasterCard. **Winter facilities:** 110 km of trails tracked and groomed for traditional and skate skiing. Back country touring on 550-acre nature preserve on Eden Mountain. **Ski shop:** equipment rental and sales, guide service, ski instruction, refreshments and lunch service, warming hut, first aid, shutle bus on weekends.

Directions: from I-91 north take exit 21 to Rte. 2 west to Rte. 15 west. In Hardwick, take Rte. 14 north for 7 miles and turn right for 3 miles to inn. From I-91 south take exit 26 to Rte. 58 west to Rte. 14 south. Go 12 miles to marked left turn, then 3 miles to inn.

NEW HAMPSHIRE

FOLLANSBEE INN, Kezar Lake, P.O. Box 92, North Sutton, NH 03260; (800) 626-4221; (603) 927-4221; Sandy and Dick Reilein, innkeepers. Open all year except for brief periods in April and November. **Rates:** $80 to $90 per double room, including breakfast. **Accommodations:** 23 rooms, 11 with private baths, 12 sharing. Dinner served family style to guests only. Service bar has beer and wine license. Children 10 and over welcome; no pets; no smoking; Visa, MasterCard. **Winter facilities:** groomed trails, ice skating, snowshoeing, ice fishing. **Ski shop** services nearby.

Directions: from I-89 south take exit 10 and follow signs to North Sutton for 2 miles. From NYC area take I-91 north to exit 10 at White River Junction to I-89 south to exit 10 as above.

MOOSE MOUNTAIN LODGE, P.O. Box 272, Etna, NH 03750; (603) 643-3529; Peter and Kay Shumway. Open Dec. 26 to March 20 and June 1 to Oct. 20. **Rates:** $75 to $95 per person double occupancy, including breakfast, lunch, and dinner. **Accommodations:** 12 rooms sharing 5 baths. Full restaurant service for guests only. BYOB. Children welcome; no pets; no smoking; Visa, MasterCard. **Winter facilities:** 50 km of trails, ice skating, snowshoeing. **Ski shop:** guide service, informal ski instruction, refreshments, warming huts, medical and first aid services in nearby Hanover.

Directions: from I-89 north take exit 18 to Rte. 120 toward Hanover for ½ mile to Etna Rd. Turn right and drive past Etna Store for ½ mile and turn right on Rudsboro Rd. for 2 miles to Dana Rd., then left on Dana for ½ mile to right turn on road to lodge.

GOLDEN EAGLE LODGE, Waterville Valley, NH 03215; (800) 468-2553; (603) 236-4551; Fax (603) 236-4174; Mark Anderson, innkeeper. Open all year. **Rates:** not available. **Accommodations:** 139 suites with private baths. Restaurant and bar facilities within walking distance. Children 12 and under free with ski week packages; no pets; some smoking allowed; Most major credit cards. **Winter facilities:** nordic ski trails and indoor pool, Jacuzzi, sauna, game room on premises. Nearby is a complete indoor sports center with tennis, running track, racquet ball, Nautilus, 25 meter pool. For recreation there is shopping, dining, entertainment in nearby Town Square.

Ski shop: equipment rental and sales, ski instruction, warming hut.

Directions: from I-93 north take exit 28 onto Rte. 49 east for 11 miles.

THE DARBY FIELD INN, P.O. Box D, Conway, NH 03818; (800) 426-4147; (603) 447-2181; Marc and Maria Donaldson, innkeepers. Open all year except the month of April. **Rates:** $82 to $92 single MAP; $124 to $164 double MAP. **Accommodations:** 1 suite and 15 rooms, all with private baths except for 2 rooms sharing. Full service restaurant and bar also provides refreshments during the day. Children 2 and over welcome; no pets; smoking limited; Spanish spoken; Visa, MasterCard, American Express. **Winter facilities:** 12 miles of private cross country trails. **Ski shop:** equipment rental and sales available in Conway.

Directions: Conway is near the Maine border in eastern New Hampshire on Rte. 16. Go ¼ mile south of intersection of Rtes. 112 and 16, turn right onto Bald Hill Rd. and go approx. 1½ miles and turn right onto dirt road for about 1 mile to inn.

THE NOTCHLAND INN, Hart's Location, NH 03812; (800) 866-6131; (603) 374-6131; Pat and John Bernardin, Innkeepers. Open all year. **Rates:** $52 to $85 per person, MAP; $75 to $100 per couple; MAP. **Accommodations:** 7 rooms, and 4 suites, all with private baths and working fireplaces. Dining room serves dinner to guests. BYOB allowed. Call about children and family rates; no pets; limited smoking; Visa, MasterCard, American Express. **Winter facilities:** 23 km tracked and groomed trails on property, open only to guests; sleigh riding; hot tub; ice skating. **Ski shop:** equipment rental by arrangement; guide service; gourmet lunches by arrangement.

Directions: from Boston take I-93 north to Rte. 3 north to Twin Mountain then go south on Rte. 302 15 miles to White Mountain National Forest.

INN AT THORN HILL, Thorn Hill Road, P.O. Box A, Jackson, NH 03846; (800) 289-8990; (603) 383-4242; Peter and Linda La Rose. Open all year except the month of April. **Rates:** $55 to $96 per person double occupancy, MAP. B&B and EP available. **Accommodations:** 15 rooms, 2 suites, 3 cabins, all with private baths except for 2 rooms sharing. Country gourmet cuisine in dining room; pub with full liquor license. Children over 12 welcome; no pets; no smoking; Spanish spoken; Visa, MasterCard, American Express. **Winter facilities:** 152 km cross country ski network starting at inn's door. Tobogganing on property. Ice skating, sleigh rides, snowshoeing, ice climbing, snowmobiling, alpine skiing nearby. **Ski shop:** equipment rental and sales, guide service, ski instruction, refreshments, medical and first aid services all available at ski touring center within walking distance of the inn.

Directions: complete directions supplied when making reservations.

PHILBROOK FARM INN, North Road, Shelburne, NH 03581; (603) 466-3831; Constance P. Leger and Nancy Philbrook, innkeepers. Open Dec. 26 to March 31 and May 1 to Oct. 31. **Rates:** $94 to $119 double, MAP. **Accommodations:** 19 rooms, 11 with private baths, 8 sharing. Dining room does not serve lunch. No bar (BYOB). Children welcome; no pets; smoking allowed; no credit cards. **Winter facilities:** ungroomed trails on property; cross country touring centers nearby. **Ski shop:** equipment rental and sales, guide service, ski instruction, and all other services and facilities available at nearby ski touring centers.

Directions: from south take I-95 north to Grey, Maine. Take Rte. 26 north to Bethel and Rte. 2 west to Shelburne. Go right at Meadow Rd. and cross bridge and take right fork in road to inn on left.

THE BALSAMS / WILDERNESS, Rte. 26, Dixville Notch, NH 03576; (800) 255-0600 [for U.S. and Canada]; (800) 255-0800 [for New Hampshire]; Fax (603) 255-4221; Warren Pearson and Stephen Barba, innkeepers. Open mid-May to mid-October and mid-December to early April. **Rates:** $75 to $140, including breakfast and skiing, varying with time of season and length of stay. **Accommodations;** 232 rooms and 5 suites, all with private baths. Dining room serves breakfast and dinner; ski area lodge has a lunch counter and coffee shop. Evening entertainment in 3 rooms: LaCave, Wilderness Lounge, Ballroom. Special programs for children; no pets; smoking in restricted areas only; French spoken; Visa, MasterCard, American Express, Discover. **Winter facilities:** Base Lodge with ski shop and school, with 60 km of cross country trails and full service alpine ski area with 12 trails, 2 slopes, and 3 lifts. There is a cross country ski center, ice skating rink, horsedrawn hayrides, and nature program. Rating from Mobil is 4 stars, and from AAA 4 diamonds. Designated as one of the Historic Hotels of America by the National Trust for Historic Preservation. **Ski shop:** equipment rental and sales, guide service, ski instruction, refreshments, warming huts, medical and first aid service.

Directions: from south (New York City and Connecticut) take I-91 north to St. Johnsbury, Vermont and Rte. 2 east to Lancaster, New Hampshire. From there take Rte. 3 north to Colebrook, NH, and Rte. 26 east to Dixville Notch. From Boston via Portsmouth, NH, take Rte. 16 north to Colebrook to Rte. 26 east to Dixville Notch. From Montreal go east on Autoroute 10 to Magog and take Rte. 55 south for 8 miles to Rte. 141 to Coaticook. From there take Rte. 147 south to Norton, VT and go east on Rte. 114 to Rte. 3 south to Colebrook and east on Rte. 26 to Dixville Notch.

MAINE

THE BETHEL INN & COUNTRY CLUB, Broad Street, Bethel, ME 04217; (800) 654-0125; (207) 824-2175; Fax (207) 824-2233; Richard D. Rasor, proprietor; Raymond G. Moran, general manager. Open all year. **Rates:** $60 per person, double occupancy, MAP. **Accommodations:** 60 rooms and 7 suites, all with private baths; 1 and 2 bedroom townhouses available, completely equipped, including washer and dryer, kitchen and tableware, overlooking cross country ski trails. Elegant country dining on verandah or in large dining rooms with fireplaces. Casual dining at Health Center's poolside lounge and at Mill Brook Tavern in main inn building. Piano bar entertainment. Excellent New England and continental cuisine with 17 entrée selections. Children welcome (under 12 stay free in parent's room); pets welcome; smoking allowed but there are non-smoking areas in dining room; French spoken; all major credit cards. **Winter facilities:** Lake house for cross country trips; year-round recreation center includes pool heated to 91°, saunas, Jacuzzi, work-out room. **Ski shop:** equipment rental and sales, guide service, ski instruction, refreshments, medical and first aid services, warming huts.

Directions: from I-95 take Maine Turnpike to exit 11 onto Rte. 26 north to Bethel (about 1 hr. driving from Turnpike exit). From New Hampshire take Rte. 2 east to Bethel.

SUNDAY RIVER INN AND CROSS COUNTRY SKI CENTER, RFD 2, Box 1688, Bethel, ME 04217; (207) 824-2410; Steve and Peggy Wight, innkeepers. Open from Thanksgiving until April 1. **Rates:** $36 to $70 per person MAP. **Accommodations:** 1 suite with private bath and 16 rooms and 5 sleeping bag dorm rooms sharing 6 baths. Family style meals served buffet style in a casual atmosphere. BYOB. Children welcome; no pets; no smoking; Visa, MasterCard, American Express. **Winter facilities:** cross country skiing on premises, ice skating, sledding; alpine skiing 1 mile away. **Ski shop:** equipment rental and sales, guide service, ski instruction, refreshments, first aid service, warming huts.

Directions: from Maine Turnpike north of Portland take exit 11 to Rte. 26 north all the way to Bethel, where it joins US-2 east. Follow signs to Sunday River on 2 east for approx. 6 miles to Sunday River Rd. and turn left to inn. From Vermont or New Hampshire, follow US-2 east to Sunday River turn-off (east of Bethel).

THE INN ON WINTER'S HILL, RR 1, Box 1272, Kingfield, ME 04947; (800) 233-WNTR; (207) 265-5421; Richard Winnick, innkeeper. Open all year. **Rates:** $75 to $139 per double room (no meals included). **Accommodations:** 19 rooms with private baths. Full service restaurant and lounge for guests. Children welcome; no pets; smoking allowed, but non-smoking rooms available; all major credit cards. **Winter facilities:** cross country skiing, ice skating, snowmobile, hot tub. Downhill skiing nearby at Sugarloaf. **Ski shop:** equipment rental and sales, guide service, ski instruction, refreshments. Medical and first aid services nearby.

Directions: from south on I-95 take exit 31B to Rte. 27 north through Farmington to Kingfield. From Montreal take Rte. 10 east to exit 121 to Rte. 55 south to exit 29 onto Rte. 108 east through North Hatley to Cookshire. From there take Rte. 212 east to Woburn and Rte. 161 south to U.S. border and Rte. 27 south to Kingfield.

LITTLE LYFORD POND CAMPS, P.O. Box 1269, Greenville, ME 04441; (207) 695-2821; Fax (207) 695-2434; Bud and Kate Fackelman, innkeepers. Open all year. **Rates:** $80 per person per day, including all meals. **Accommodations:** 7 cabins, each with private outhouse. No bar facilities (BYOB). Children acceptable; no pets; smoking outside only; no credit cards. **Winter facilities:** 60 km of marked and cleared back country trails. Sauna. **Ski shop:** nothing formal except that repairs can be made; bring all your own equipment.

Directions: Fly in from Greenville. The 13 mile ski-in from Greenville is only for the very tough and experienced.

QUEBEC

HOVEY MANOR, Hovey Road, P.O. Box 60, North Hatley, Québec J0B 2C0, Canada; (819) 842-2421; Fax (819) 842-2248; Stephen J. Stafford, innkeeper; Open all year. **Rates:** $95 to $145 per person per night (double occupancy) MAP (including gratuities). Discounted 3, 5, 7 night packages available. **Accommodations:** 35 rooms with private baths, many with fireplaces, Jacuzzis, and canopied beds. Dining room serves lunch and dinner to public as well as guests (lunch 12–2 P.M., dinner 6–9:30 P.M.). Fully licensed. Children welcome—those sleeping in parents room at ½ rate; no pets; smoking allowed; Visa, MasterCard, American Express, Diners Club. Winter facilities: 35 km of groomed cross country trails, waxing room, skating

rink, deluxe ice fishing cabins, games room, indoor tennis, squash, racquet ball, curling, Olympic pool nearby.

Directions: from Montreal take *Pont* Champlain Bridge to Autoroute 10 (*Autoroute des Cantons de l'est*). From Rte. 10 take exit (*sortie*) 121 to Rte. 55 south (*sud*) to exit 29 to North Hatley on Rte. 108 east (*est*) and follow signs to Hovey Manor entrance. From Vermont take I-91 north to Canadian border and follow Rte. 55 north to North Hatley exit (exit 29) onto Rte. 108 east and follow signs to inn.

AUBERGE HANDFIELD, 555 Richelieu, St-Marc-sur-le-Richelieu, Québec J0L 2E0, Canada: (514) 584-2226; Fax (514) 584-3650; Conrad Handfield, innkeeper. Open all year. **Rates:** $55 to $145 double, not including meals. **Accommodations:** 55 rooms, 11 suites, 8 cabins, all with private baths. Breakfast, lunch, and dinner served in dining room. There is also a bar and lounge. Children welcome; no pets; smoking allowed; English and French spoken. **Winter facilities:** cross country skiing, alpine skiing, ice skating, spa and health club.

Directions: from Montreal take Autoroute 20 east towards Quebec City to exit 112 onto Rte. 223 north for 10 km (6 miles) to inn.

HÔTEL LE CHANTECLER, 1474 Chemin Chantecler, C.P. 1048, Ste-Adèle, Québec J0R 1L0, Canada; (800) 363-2420; Fax (514) 229-5593; Georges Delaney, president and general manager. Open all year. **Rates:** from $129 single and from $179 double, MAP. **Accommodations:** 280 rooms, 20 suites, 7 cabins, all with private baths. Full service main dining room, 2 cafeterias, 3 bars. Children welcome, no pets; smoking allowed; English and French spoken; Visa, MasterCard, American Express, Diners Club, Carte Blanche, En Route. **Winter facilities:** guests can ski on the resort only, or they can also ski farther afield off the resort. There is a network of cross country trails and daily activities. There are 4 mountains, 8 lifts, 22 trails, 13 of which are lighted, and snow-making equipment. **Ski shop:** equipment rental and sales, guide service, ski instruction, refreshments at the 2 cafeterias, 2 boutiques for shopping, nursery.

Directions: from Montreal, take Autoroute 15 to exit 67 and follow instructions the hotel will give you when making reservations. Ask also about hotel's mini bus service and transportation from Dorval and Mirabel airports.

LE CHÂTEAU MONTEBELLO, 392 Notre Dame, Montebello, Québec J0V 1L0, Canada; (819) 423-6341; Fax (819) 423-5283; Jacques Ternois, general manager. Open all year. **Rates:** $245 double, including all meals. **Accommodations:** 210 rooms, 16 suites, all with private baths. Aux Chantignoles is the main dining room, in addition to Café des Nations and Bar Excalibur. Children welcome; no pets; English and French spoken; all major credit cards. **Winter facilities:** 60 km cross country ski trails, snowshoeing, ice fishing, snowmobiling, sleigh rides, indoor pool, whirlpool, sauna. **Ski shop:** equipment rental and sales, guide service, ski instruction, refreshments, medical and first aid services.

Directions: located on Rte. 148 half way between Montreal and Ottawa.

FAR HILLS INN, Val Morin, Québec J0T 2R0, Canada; (800) 567-6636; (819) 322-2014 or (514) 866-2219; Fax (819) 322-1995; David and Louise Pemberton Smith, innkeepers. Open all year. **Rates:** $99 to $119 per person MAP; weekly ski packages, including instruction, as low as $89 per person per night. **Accommodations:** 72 rooms with private baths. Dining room serves breakfast, lunch, and dinner to guests and public. Liquor served in the Panorama Lounge with live entertain-